A First Poetry Book

Pie Corbett has advised the National Literacy Strategy for both the Primary and Key Stage 3 phase. He works across the country running inset and development projects, and was co-leader of the DfES Innovations project on 'Storymaking', based at the International Learning and Research Centre. Author of over 250 books, he writes poetry, stories and materials for teachers. He has compiled many bestselling anthologies for Macmillan Children's Books, including *The Works 2*, *The Works 4* and *Assembly Poems*. This is his first solo collection for children.

Gaby Morgan is the Editorial Director of the Macmillan Children's Books poetry list. She has edited a number of bestselling anthologies, including *Read Me: A Poem for Every Day of the Year* and *Christmas Poems*. She lives in Hampshire with Grant, Jude and Evie.

Another book by Pie Corbett

Evidence of Dragons

Another book chosen by Gaby Morgan

Puppy Poems

MACMILLAN
POETRY

A First Poetry Book

Pie Corbett and Gaby Morgan

MACMILLAN CHILDREN'S BOOKS

First published 2012 by Macmillan Children's Books
a division of Macmillan Publishers Limited
20 New Wharf Road, London N1 9RR
Basingstoke and Oxford
Associated companies throughout the world
www.panmacmillan.com

ISBN 978-0-330-54374-3

3 5 7 9 8 6 4 2

A CIP catalogue record for this book is available from
the British Library.

Printed and bound by CPI Group (UK) Ltd, Croydon CR0 4YY

Contents

MONSTERS, MYTHICAL CREATURE AND DINOSAURS

NATURE

SEASONS AND WEATHER

SENSES

THE PAST

THE SEASIDE

Introduction

My earliest poems were scraps of nursery rhymes and songs. This comforting store of language provided me with a bank of soothing patterns and strange images. Cows that jumped over the moon and old ladies who lived in shoes littered my imagination. I heard these rhymes so often that soon they became part of my store of special language.

Once I arrived in school, the poetry store was soon added to by a wide variety of playground rhymes. Some were mysterious, while others were used in the games that we played. In lessons we learned different sorts of rhymes and poems. Some of these I still know, after over half a century. They have stayed inside me as an important part of my memory bank of language and pictures, a mingling of sounds and meaning.

Poems are experiences – to be spoken aloud and savoured. Some will leave you cold, while others create an echo. Perhaps these will stay with you forever. This collection is packed with poems for children to listen to, read aloud and perform. Why not paint pictures to illustrate them, invent musical patterns and dances to accompany performances? Talk about what they suggest – the memories they trigger and feelings that surround them.

Let the poems become little shafts of sunlight to brighten up the day. Fifty years ago, a teacher let

Blake's Tyger loose into my imaginative world. It is still there, stalking through the darkness, staring at me with fiery eyes. We have travelled many miles since then, but every time I read that poem the tiger gets up, shakes its amazing body and starts to prowl. So, let a few tigers loose into the imagination. There is room enough.

Pie Corbett 2012

FAIRIES, MERMAIDS AND PRINCESSES

The Princess's Treasures

The Princess owned a whole turret of
  treasures.

There was a toy dragon that breathed
  real sparks,
A necklace made from the stony tears
  of statues,
A wooden unicorn that danced on a
  lawn of green glass,
A casket of blue shells from a
  mermaid's cave
And a tiny spinning wheel
That could turn spider silk into birdsong.

Yet the thing she loved the best
Was a scruffy crimson rug.

Its patterns had been stolen by the
    desert sun,
Its fringes had been frayed by ice
    storms,
Its tufts had been flattened by sleeping
    tigers,
But still it rippled across her room
Like an ancient flying fish,
And when it slept beside her bed
It smelled of spices
And meadow flowers
And salty seas.

                              Clare Bevan

I Am a Princess

Hello.
I am pleased to meet you
I am a princess
And I have a lot of rules
Which you must obey

Whenever you see me
You must bow or curtsy

You must never argue with me
Because a princess is always right

You must never wear a dress
That is prettier than mine

I choose the game we will play
And it is always my turn first

Remember. You are very lucky
To be playing with me

And I have to win every game

But before you go
Could you please explain
Why I have no friends?

Roger Stevens

Listen and Look

Winds whistle,
waves whisper
stories on the shore;
tales of treasure,
men and mermaids,
galleons and gore.

Night comes;
in the moonlight
sands are silver strands,
dream ways,
gleam ways
washed by magic hands.

See the sparkle,
hear the stories,
hold them in your head.
Memories are more
than moments,
words are more
than letters read.

Patricia Leighton

Monisha

Each afternoon
at playgroup
when it's one o'clock
I get my favourite things
from the dressing-up box,
the crown, the cape, the fairy's wings,
the gold mask for my eyes,
and I become
Monisha,
Princess of the Skies.

Each afternoon
at playgroup
when it's three o'clock
I put on what I came in,
my tracksuit, shoes and socks,
and when I've finished changing
I say all my bye-byes,
and I am now Monisha,
a princess in disguise.

David Horner

A Few Frightening Things

These are the things a Princess fears . . .

Broken mirrors,
Dragon tears,
Poisoned apples,
Wicked wands,
Slimy frogs
In slimy ponds,
Rusty keys
For creaky locks,
Stinging nettles,
Silent clocks,
Sharpened combs
By haunted wells,
Spinning wheels
And cruel spells,
Sleeping for
A hundred years . . .

These are the things a Princess fears.

Clare Bevan

Fairy Names

What shall we call the Fairy Child?

Mouse-Fur? Cat's Purr?
Weasel-Wild?

Bat-Wing? Bee-Sting?
Shining River?
Snakebite? Starlight?
Stone? Or Shiver?

Acorn? Frogspawn?
Golden Tree?
Snowflake? Daybreak?
Stormy Sea?

Snail-Shell? Harebell?
Scarlet Flame?

How shall we choose the Fairy's name?

Clare Bevan

Where the Fairies Are

Wild laughter, tiny wingbeats
Ripples on the lake
Whispers chatter through the
    hedgerows
Springtime fairies wake.

Gentle heat-haze on the meadows
Floats across the sky
From cowslip bells and dandelions
Summer fairies fly.

Frosted nights and golden sunlight
Woodsmoke scents the day
Falling leaves flame red and orange
Autumn fairies play.

Snow and ice freeze up the farmland
Silent, drifting deep
Far away inside the forests
Winter fairies sleep.

David Harmer

Never Pick a Fight with a Fairy

Never pick a fight with a fairy
She may seem insubstantial and airy
But her magic is such
That with just one light touch
She could turn you to jelly. That's scary

Roger Stevens

The Faery Ferry

The evening looms late, the stars are on
  fire,
the sun has departed, the moon climbs
  higher.

The insects are airborne, the day is
  retreating,
the ravens are resting, a dark heart is
  beating.

The trees sigh and settle, the hedges
  catnapping,
The rush of the river slows to a
  slapping.

The skin of an apple, the coat of a
  berry
catch a sparkle of light from the faery
  ferry.

John Rice

The Mermaids in the Sea

The mermaids in the sea are
Far hardier than we are;
And in the summer wear
Only the gilded air;
The blue translucencies
And foam-lace of the seas.
But when the seas are rough
They put on sailors' stuff:
Garments that seamen wore
Who never reached a shore.
They sit on rocks and crunch
An oceanic lunch.
They suck on bones and ribs,
They smack their salty lips
Above their sailor-bibs.

Gerda Mayer

Mermaid's Purse

In my purse I keep
A mother- of- pearl comb
For my seaweed hair,
A hollow shell to phone the sea
To check for ships
A magic crystal to give me legs for
A day so I can climb over rocks
To peep at the farmyard over the hill,
A pirate's doubloon I dived for
Buried down in the sandy seabed
Near an ancient barnacled shipwreck,
A baby fish, my faithful pet,
A crab shell containing coconut oil
To polish my scales,
A necklace of pearls,
A razor shell to etch mysterious
    messages in the sand,
A starfish to remind me of the skies at
    night
When I swim into my cave to see out
    wild storms,
A shark's tooth for luck,
A small green glass bottle, corked,

Containing eastern oils from far away
This to sip and soothe my siren calls
Summoning sailors on the oceans wide.
And, last, moonbeams to light my way
In the midnight blue swirling world that
  is my home.

Kate Sedgwick

Tales

Tall tales
high as the mast,
pieces of gale
the sailor brought home from sea.

Small tales
carried in grandmother's
pocket, in the flowered
apron of time. Strands of bright wool.

Pretty tales
told to plain children:
once there was
Good Luck, and Good Luck won;

And married Good Looks
and they begot Good Nature.
Happy princes!
They're living yet.

                              Gerda Mayer

FAMILIES

Jellybean, Bellybean

Jellybean, Bellybean
Curled up small,
Sometimes I wonder
If you're there at all.

Jillybean, Billybean,
Soon we'll see
How you unfurl and grow,
Baby-to-be.

Sue Cowling

My Baby Sister

A small red face,
a button nose,
starfish hands
and tiny toes.
She has no hair,
her eyes are bright
and she was only
born last night.
Mum let me hold her
which was fun.
Now I'm not
the only one.

Marian Swinger

Freddie's Little Sister

My friend Freddie's little sister
thinks she's a dog.

She sits in the dog basket,
underneath the kitchen worktop,
and barks.

"What are you doing?"
I ask.
"Woof, woof."
she says.

She eats dog biscuits.
Not just the little round ones,
but the long ones shaped like a bone.

"It's on account of us
getting a dog at the same time
she was born."
says Freddie's mum,
throwing her another dog biscuit.
"It's no problem, really."

The dog never says anything.
Just sits there,
his head on his paws,
and looks sad.

One day
Freddie's little sister
bit the postman on the leg.

"Right."
said Freddie's dad.
"This has gone far enough.
You are not a dog.
Do you understand?
YOU ARE NOT A DOG!"

Freddie's little sister nodded,
climbed on to the kitchen worktop,
curled up and said,
"Miaow!"

Robin Mellor

Baby Brother

Baby Brother
Blanket Hugger
Finger Gripper
Paper Ripper
Rusk Nibbler
Spit Dribbler
Food Slurper
Champion Burper!

Baby Brother
Teddy Lover
Toy Breaker
Playpen Shaker
Juice Spiller
Nappy Filler
Tummy Wriggler
Champion Giggler!

Baby Brother
Thumb Sucker
Toe Sucker
Foot Sucker
Foot Kicker
Nose Picker
Peek-a-boo Peeper
Champion Sleeper!

Celia Gentles

It's the Cougar in the Hoover

Can you clean the bathroom floor?

ash
Mum, I know we Sp l   a bit, spl
        ed
               ash shh sh
but the ships were racing in the basin
and the water didn't fit.

Can you clear up
the biscuit crumbs where you had a
*   midnight feast?*

Mum, there's a cougar in the hoover
and he bares his grrrrrrreat big teeth –
(and he means it!).

Could you lay the table? Dinner's ready
*   soon . . .*

A spoooooooooonbill stole the knives and
    forks,
and flew back to the zooooo.

Please take your bicycles
off the garden path.

But there's a giraffe asleep right next to
    them
snoring on the grass
(giraffe-length snores like this:
ZZZZZZZZZZZZZZZzzzzzz).

Excuse me, is that your uniform
underneath the bed?

Yes, a unicorn is using it
for a nest instead.

Well, inform the unicorn
you need to iron it for school.

But, Mum, you surely know
to inform a unicorn's uncool
                    uncool
                      uncool!

                    Judith Green

My Face Says It All!

When I've made mischief
Or my tale's been tall,
My mum always knows
Cos my face says it all.
Well . . . that's what my mum says
Then I'm in disgrace,
I wish I could learn
How to silence my face!

Philip Waddell

My Mum

Glasses wearer,
Great carer,
Wants it neater,
But so sweet-er,
Promise keeper,
Car-horn beeper,
Book maker,
Child creator.

Evie Weston

My Dad

My dad's not a teacher,
a ghost or a ghoul,
he isn't a spaceman,
a jester or fool.

He doesn't walk tightropes
or dance on hot coals,
play for United
or score lots of goals.

He isn't a rock star,
a wizard or king,
he isn't a builder
and he can't really sing.

He doesn't do time walks
or cook on TV,
write silly poems
or make cups of tea.

My dad isn't wealthy,
he's not strong or wild,
but my dad is special
and I am his child.

Peter Dixon

Gran's Old Diary

I found my gran's old diary,
it has a lock and key.
I found it in the attic,
when you explored with me.

My gran wrote her old diary
many years ago.
She used the blackest ink
on pages white as snow.

And inside Gran's old diary
something caught my eye:
it was a tiny buttercup
pressed flat from years gone by.

Wes Magee

Driving Home

Coming back home from Granny's in
  the car
I try to stay awake. I really do.
I look around to find the evening star
And make a wish. Who knows? It might
  come true.

I watch the yellow windows whizzing by
And sometimes see a person in a room,
Cutting a loaf of bread, tying a tie,
Stretching, or watching telly in the
  gloom.

I see the street lamps flash past, one by
  one,
And watch how people's shadows
  grow and shrink.
It's like a trick; I wonder how it's done.
I breathe and watch, and settle back
  to think.

But everything gets mixed and far
   away;
I feel I'm moving but I don't know
   where.
I hear a distant voice which seems to
   say,
"Wake up! (She's fast asleep.) Wake
   up! We're there!"

Gerard Benson

My Baby Brother's Secrets

When my baby brother
wants to tell me a secret,
he comes right up close.
But instead of putting his lips
against my ear,
he presses his ear
tightly against my ear.
Then, he whispers so softly
that I can't hear
a word he is saying.

My baby brother's secrets
are safe with me.

John Foster

FEELINGS

Lullaby

I will weave you a web
Of words, my love,
To whisper you to sleep.

I will tell you a tale
Of dolphins and whales
And not leave you counting sheep.

And in your sleep
The words will shape
Your brightly coloured dreams

That float from your head
And surround your bed
Until you wake safely again.

David Greygoose

Something on the Carpet

I nearly stepped in something
on the carpet;
retraced my steps till my shoe sank
into a small patch of sunlight.

Now I am walking sunshine
all over the house.

Celia Warren

The Quiet Things

When I want to escape from talk and
    to-do
Then these are the quiet things I do:
Sit with a book in the crook of a tree
To read of far places like Trincomalee,
With islands and pirates – and then
    perhaps
Draw some imaginary treasure maps;
Lie in long grass staring up at the sky
As white cotton-wool clouds drift easily
    by
Or out in the garden pass long sunny
    hours
Watching fat bumblebees fumbling at
    flowers;
Chat with our cat: in her gentle way
I'm sure she agrees with all that I say;
Or talk with our goldfish (one's actually
    black):
You can tell at a glance that they're
    talking back.

Then stand by the waterfall quite close
   to home
Tranced by smooth water and dancing
   white foam . . .

All quiet things – oh, and this too:
Whispering plans and secrets with you.

Eric Finney

Jealousy

Jealousy was a feeling
I always tried to hide
But then it got a hold on me
And ate me up inside.

It made me feel unhappy
It made me feel unkind
And though I wished it would go away
It was always on my mind.

Jealousy only left me
Once I understood
That it never makes things better
And does no one any good.

John Mole

Moody

Blue
is my mood today.
And grey
like the falling rain.

I'm red
when I'm angry,
purple, in pain.
Green is for jealousy,
black for despair
when the world's not fair.

But I'm not such
a misery
as you might think.
Sometimes
I'm tickled

pink.

Ann Bonner

Happy

I'm as happy as a rainbow,
Or a dolphin in the sea.
As happy as a kangaroo,
Or a buzzy bee.
As happy as a flip-flop
Walking in the sand.
As happy as a big bass drum
In the happy band.

Michaela Morgan

First Glasses

Blink and blink again

like butterfly wings
against a windowpane.

Paul Henry

Imagine the World

Give me a box of colours
and I'll paint a magic land,
with rainbows spanning purple hills,
green seas and golden sand.

Give me a pot of pencils
and I'll write fantastic words,
poems about secret forests,
shy squirrels and soaring birds.

Give me a book of music
and I'll sing a fabulous song
to keep the people happy
and smiling all day long.

Give me a packet of seeds
and I'll make a garden grow
with poppies, pinks and petunias,
blooming row upon row.

Make and bake, plant and paint,
imagine a world brand new.
Write magic words, sing magic songs,
till our rainbow world comes true.

Moira Andrew

Days

I have this great feeling inside me,
Bubbling and fizzing away,
That today will be bright
And full of sunlight,
A happy and glorious day.

I have this sad feeling inside me,
Weighing me down like a stone,
That today will be grey
And gloomy all day,
A dingy and miserable day.

I have this calm feeling inside me,
Soothing me like a soft song,
That today will be warm
Without any storm,
A quiet, quite ordinary day.

John Foster

Where Am I?

I'm not feeling happy.
I'm not feeling sad.
I'm exactly halfway between
Gloomy and glad.

I'm not one or the other.
I'm not up, I'm not down.
I'm not smiling a smile.
I'm not frowning a frown.

I'm somewhere in the middle.
A new place I've invented.
It doesn't seem to have a name,
I'm just perfectly contented.

Mike Barfield

Sad-Happy

A smile after tears
like sun shining through showers
makes life a rainbow.

Jane Clarke

Mood-Walking

When I'm fed up I walk like this:
stamp, stomp, barge, bang, bump,
    thump, crash!

But when I'm cheered up, I walk like
    this:
swish, swirl, spin, twirl, skip, jump, boing!

What about you?

Kate Williams

FOOD

The Alphabite

Apple pie, sausage, potato, salmon,
Bramble, chives, porridge,
    marshmallow, gammon,
Cabbage, peas, jacket spud,
    chocolate log, crab,
Doughnut, cheese, Yorkshire pud, hot
    dog, kebab,
Egg, nut roast, pizza, bun, bubble and
    squeak,
Fig pudding, buttered toast, fajita,
    scone, leek,
Grapefruit, aubergine, custard, fruit
    flan,
Honey, tangerine, mustard, meringue,
Ice lolly, chops, tagliatelle, tomato,
Jam, broccoli, baps, thyme, avocado,
Ketchup, goose, cannelloni, eclair,
Lemon mousse, macaroni, plum
    pudding, pear,
Melon, tortilla chip, black cherry, yam,
Noodle, satsuma, crisp, raspberry jam,
Olive, aubergine, marmalade, chilli,

Parsnip, tangerine, mushroom, grape,
  jelly,
Quiche, fish finger, pepper, hash,
  mussel,
Rhubarb fool, lettuce, goulash, Brussels
Sprouts, fondue, mangetout, scampi,
  banana,
Treacle tart, Irish stew, pasty, sultana,
Ugli fruit, ravioli, cucumber, steak,
Vol-au-vent, roly-poly, soup, sponge
  cake,
Waffle, crumble, salad, hotpot, hot
X buns, pumpkin, celery, apricot,
Yogurt, spaghetti, rice, biscuit, baked
  bean,
Zabaglione, pitta, fritter, ice cream.

David Horner

Apple

i
hold an apple
in my hand. It feels so
smooth, all red and round.
I smell the apple's fruity zing.
I lick the skin and bite right
in. My tongue delights
in fruit so ripe. Crisp.
Tangy. Apple!

James Carter

A Rainbow of Fruit Flavours

Red raspberry ripple
Orange clementine tang
Yellow melon squelch
Green apple crunch
Blue blueberry burst
Indigo grape escape
Violet plum punch
A rainbow of fruit flavours

Paul Cookson

Poem in Praise of
My Favourite Vegetable

The

pea

is

for

me

!

Bernard Young

Beans v Peas

Beans are much more tasty,
And save all the time I'm wasting
Chasing peas around my plate.

Celina Macdonald

Pancake Chant

Two, four, six, eight,
If you want some, grab a plate!
Eight, two, four, six,
You can toss them while I mix.
Four, six, eight, two,
Lemon? Syrup? Which are you?
Six, eight, two, four,
Always room for just one more
P-A-N-C-A-K-E . . . Pancake!

Sue Cowling

Cream Curdled Oceans

Cream curdled oceans lick
The salt from
Sugar dusted rocks
The caramel nut covered sand
Lies across fudge filled earth.
The chocolate gulls fly
Around the lashings of candyfloss
    clouds
Stretched across endless miles of
Honey drenched sky.
In the distance
There are cocoa moulded mountains
Covered with
Peppermint gum trees,
Custard carved boats
Sail to candy cane lighthouses,
That light up the beach
With their gumball beacons.
Shortbread crabs creep past
Into lemonade rock pools
Jelly seaweed is scattered
Across the land,
Surrounded by shells of biscotti.

Violet Macdonald

Tummy Traveller

We went to Yorkshire for the puddings
Melton Mowbray for the pies.
Lush leeks we liked in Wales,
In Stilton cheese supplies.
We went to Lancashire for hotpot,
Devon for cream teas.
Scotland meant a haggis,
Cumberland – sausage, please
We went to Grimsby for a kipper,
Cornish pasties, with some peas,
Kent for juicy apples
– No more, if you please!

Redvers Brandling

53

Peter's Pizzas

When Peter picks a pizza
he creates a work of art,
choosing grated cheese, tomatoes,
and onions for a start.

He says he'll have a slice of ham,
and garlicky salami,
and shredded chicken, strips of beef,
enough to feed an army.

He likes some fine-chopped
    mushrooms,
and peppers – red and green –
and when you think he's made
the biggest pizza ever seen,

he asks for flakes of tuna,
for prawns and bits of squid,
asparagus and olives –
he's a very greedy kid.

When Peter picks a pizza
he empties half the shop,
for a pizza's not a pizza
till a banquet sits on top.

Alison Chisholm

Untraditional Pasty

Once,
   inside a pasty
   I discovered a small seagull –
   plus:
         peas, potatoes
         turnip (sliced)
         herbs and feathers
         nicely diced
It shook its wings
it gave a cry
and swiftly flew into the sky.
   I watched it soar
   swoop and glide
   – and wondered how
   it got inside
   a pasty
   from a Cornish shop
   crisp and juicy
   piping hot.
I'll never know . . .
But they do say:
"Strange things happen Cornwall way."

Peter Dixon

FRIENDS

My Friends

My friends are

Funny, faithful, freaky
Ready to stand by me
Interested in what I do
Easy with what I say
Never too busy to help
Dead keen to share in the games I play
Sometimes open, sometimes sneaky

but still my friends, so that's OK

Phil Rampton

Cowboys and Indians

This morning me and my friends played
   cowboys and Indians.
It was really fun! We made bows and
   arrows
And Jimmy pretended to be a horse.
Then we all ran around shouting while
   Azeem chased us
And then they tied me to a tree.
We were all having lots of fun, shouting
   and stuff,
When Mum called us in for tea and
   biscuits.

I really like playing cowboys and
   Indians;
But it's getting dark out here.

Violet Macdonald

Wisdom

Behind the sofa, hand in hand,
we hide from fee-fis,
foes and fums,
passing tigers,
hissing snakes,
alligators, growling bears.

We have built ourselves a cave,
   mainly cushions,
   partly coats,
   piles of papers,
   legs of chairs.

And here we lie
in cuddled arms,
warm and cosy
free from harm.

Hand in hand we hear the bear,
clutch of fingers, gasp of fear.

"We are safe in the cave,"
I whisper.
Comes a silence,
"They live in caves,"
comes his reply.

Peter Dixon

my cat doesn't love

my cat doesn't love
　　sardines for his tea
as much as he loves me

my cat doesn't love
　　sardines for his tea
　　or saucers full of cream
as much as he loves me

my cat doesn't love
　　sardines for his tea
　　or saucers full of cream
　　or bird-watch on TV
as much as he loves me

my cat doesn't love
　　sardines for his tea
　　or saucers full of cream
　　or bird-watch on TV
　　or scratching for his fleas
as much as he loves me

my cat doesn't love
    sardines for his tea
    or saucers full of cream
    or bird-watch on TV
    or scratching for his fleas
    or dancing in his dreams
as much as he loves me

my cat doesn't love
    sardines for his tea
    or saucers full of cream
    or bird-watch on TV
    or scratching for his fleas
    or dancing in his dreams
    or purring on your knee
as much as he loves me

he loves me best, you see

Danielle Sensier

Different But the Same

Jo's tall. **I'm small.**
She's vegetarian. **I eat meat.**
She's a swimmer. **I'm an acrobat.**
She's got gerbils. **I've got a rat.**
She has a sister. **I have a brother.**
We're totally different **from each other!**

But in a way, we're just the same.
We always agree which game to play,
and whatever she says, I was going
to say,
and everything we say makes us
giggle away.
So we're not really different at all!

Kate Williams

Friend

Arm linker
Eye winker
Time sparer
Treat sharer.

Hand lender
Defender
Word taker
Peacemaker.

Word keeper
Praise heaper
High fiver
Reviver.

Philip Waddell

Everything's Better with You

jokes are much funnier
holidays sunnier
everything's better with you

biscuits are crunchier
popcorn is munchier
bananas are bunchier
everything's better with you

homework is easier
life's bright and breezier
pizza is cheesier
ice cream is freezier
everything's better with you

sherbet is fizzier
buzzing bees busier
fairground rides dizzier
questions are quizzier
frisbees are whizzier
everything's better with you

colours are zingier
microwaves pingier
church bells are ringier
gold chains are blingier
and you're just humdingier
super song singier
everything's better with you
oh everything's better with you

Jan Dean

Moving House

This is the very last day
that I'll be in Class Three.
Tomorrow we're moving away
to a big house near the sea.

I've packed up everything
for the men to put in the van,
but I do wish I could bring
my very best friend Dan.

My new school's really great,
the teacher was kind to me.
The kids all smiled and I can't wait
to see who my friend will be.

"You can have a pet," says Dad,
"and a slide in the garden too."
But I still feel a little bit sad.
Dan, who will be playing with you?

Jo Peters

Picking Poppies

I pictured picking poppies,
Picking poppies, that was me;
I'd pop out to pick poppies,
In the poppy patch I'd be.
In the poppies I'm a-picking,
With my best friend Patsy Peft,
I've been out a-picking poppies,
Oh, but now there's nothing left.

Violet Macdonald

Anything

Anything that's broken
I will mend.

Anything that needs to go
I will send.

Anytime you call me
I will attend.

You can ask me anything.
I am your friend.

Bernard Young

Oops

Careless Chloe made a promise
But in minutes she had dropped it;
There it lay, smashed to pieces.
Chloe's mates all helped their friend
Try to fix the bits together
But (and I imagine you are
Wise and may already know this)
Broken promises don't mend.

Frances Nagle

Twins?

We're hard to pull apart,
we stick to each other like glue.
I gave her mumps and measles,
she gave me her dose of the flu.

If she asks to visit the toilet
then I must go there too.
If I can't puzzle out my sums,
she shows me what to do

If there's a fight I'll protect her;
she does the same for me.
I hold her hand in assembly,
we sing in harmony.

She passes me notes in class
with her name and mine in a heart.
They say we must be twins –
we're never seen apart

I'm sure there'll never be anyone else
I'd rather have round to play.
If she really were my sister, Mum says,
we'd probably fight all day!

Brian Moses

MINIBEASTS

Diary of a Butterfly

Chomp, chomp, chomp, chomp,
  chomp;
safe, secure, silk-spun stillness;
flap, flap, flap, flap, flap.

Mike Johnson

Whelks and Winkles

Whelks and winkles
  cockles too
do not have a lot to do.
They sit around from day to day
watching beachfolk
dance and play.

But come the winter
  mighty seas
wrecks and wreckings
  icy breeze . . .
Whilst other moan
and sailors struggle,
whelks and winkles
  sleep and cuddle . . .
  seashell houses,
  strong and warm,
  safe from wind
  and winter's storm.

                    Peter Dixon

Small Mysteries

Morning
birdybrekkus
longbody, pinkling
wigglestring

gentle earthshift
facefree, soileater
underneather

Afternoon
roundabout birdlady
dot, dot, dot, dot, dot

busylady, shinybird
red, black, red.

rubybird, fly, walk
rose stem, bud

Evening
velvet-greyself
moonridden, hawksoft
featherface

lamplove, tap, tap, tap
dusty, wrigglechild
munchcloth

Night
Ms F. Bitehoppy
Fur House
No. 1, Leaping Lane,
Dogtown, Scratchin
1TCH ED

Mandy Coe

busy beeing lazy

he surfs
a current of air
puzzles
(no rush)
about where
to go next

he smells
a nuzzly
nectary scent
hovers
above orange
yellow and red

he glides
in hazily
flops to a stop
on a breath-soft
powdered pillow
of pollen

he sinks
in softly
lazily bathes
in a drowsy haze
of feathery
stamens

he lifts
himself up
a bundle of fluff
a buzzing
blaze
of rusty fuzz

he surfs
a current of air
puzzles
(no rush)
about where
to go next

Lynne Taylor

I Like Minibeasts

I like worms and snails and slugs,
I like beetles, I like bugs,
I like ladybirds, and earwigs too,
I like dragonflies, green and blue.
I like spiders and butterflies,
I like stag beetles, monster-sized
I like minibeasts, they're such fun
but my brother doesn't like them.
Watch him run.

Marian Swinger

Who Am I?
(A kenning)

Stripy pullover
Sharp stinger
Buzzing buzzer
Honey bringer

Paul Cookson

(A bee)

Newborn

Crack open chrysalis
Come into the light
Stretch wet wings
Prepare for your first flight.
Wait for a warm breeze
To lift you way up high
Brand-new butterfly
Fly into the sky.

Catharine Boddy

Red Admiral

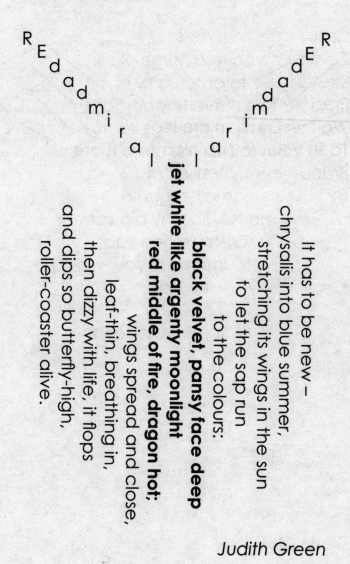

R E d a d m i r a l   l a r i m d a a d E R

It has to be new –
chrysalis into blue summer,
stretching its wings in the sun
to let the sap run

to the colours:

black velvet, pansy face deep
jet white like argenty moonlight
red middle of fire, dragon hot;

wings spread and close,
leaf-thin, breathing in,
then dizzy with life, it flops
and dips so butterfly-high,
roller-coaster alive.

Judith Green

Spider-Man

I
weave a home of silk
to catch a fly or
two, I'm a tiny acrobat
I have eight legs it's true
But to me you are a giant
And I'm
smaller than a
mouse, So why did you
scream when you
found me in your
house?

Sue Hardy-Dawson

The Climber

See him climbing up the wall,
Step by step I watch him crawl,
Leg by leg he feels his way
Through the shadows of the day.
At the ceiling he will stop,
Cast his threads and start to drop
Down and down, he knows no failure,
Expert climber and abseiler.

Coral Rumble

Who Am I?

sticky knitter
scary scurrier
tricky tangler
leggy spinner
trap ease artist
blob with legs on
ogling octo-ped
web sight

Philip Burton

(A spider)

Ladybird

Red round ladybird
in the flowerpots,
walking up the leafy stems
in your polka dots,

twice as nice and useful
despite your tiny size,
you decorate the garden
and eat up all the flies!

Liz Brownlee

Minibeasts

Riddle

I'm two inches long and shiny black.
I can give a painful bite.
I look rather fierce and some people
    think I'm a fighter.
That's because I've got antlers like a
    deer.
My jaws are strong and sharp. And
    though I'm big,
I'm not as big as an African Goliath
    Beetle,
which is five inches long. That makes
    me think
I'm not so big after all.

What am I?

Katherine Gallagher

(A stag beetle)

MONSTERS, MYTHICAL CREATURES AND DINOSAURS

The Monster Under
Your Bed

Don't shout at the monster
Under your bed –

It's terribly lonely,
It's never been fed,
It can't fool around,
And it can't make a noise,
Its friends are the beetles
And old, broken toys.

It sleeps in a tangle
Of tissues and socks,
Its voice is as soft
As the ticking of clocks,
It's not like the monsters
Who lurk in your dreams,
It's frightened of footsteps,
And slippers, and screams.
It's tiny and timid,
It's green, pink and blue,
It's under your bed, and . . .

It's hiding from YOU!

Clare Bevan

My Newt

I found it in the playground
Looking very cute.
I took it to my teacher
Who said, "It's called a newt."

She put it in a fish tank
And fed it every day.
It grew and grew. "That's strange," she
    said.
"Whatever does it weigh?"

It ate as much as forty dogs,
Drank water by the flagon.
The Head came in to have a look,
Said, "Newt? THAT is a DRAGON!"

She called the Head of Fairy Tales
To take the beast away.
It lives now in a deep, dark cave
With jewels on display.

Pam Gidney

Beware of the . . . ?

Diving from the starry sky,
Roaring loudly, soaring high,
Awful flames and awful heat,
Golden scales and spiky feet,
Over wood and castle wall . . .
Not a friendly beast at all!

Clare Bevan

Fossils

Frozen in time
Over millions of years
Snapshots of an ancient age
Skeletons held
In Earth's hard depths
Like nature's long-kept
Secrets

Graham Denton

What Are *Dinos* Made Of?

Grr! Grr! Grr!

Grr!Grr!Grr!

Grr!

Grr!Grr!

Grr!

Grr!

Grr!

Grr!

Grr!

Grr!   Grr!   Grr!

Grr!Grr!Grr!Grr!

Grr!   Grr!   Grr!

Grr!Grr!

Grr!Grr!Grr!

Grr!Grr!Grr!Grr!

Grr!Grr!Grr!Grr!Grr!   Grr!

Grr!Grr!Grr!Grr!   Grr!   Grr!

Grr!   Grr!   Grr!   Grr!

Grr!   Grr!   Grr!

Grr!   Grr!

Grr!   Grr!

Grr!Grr!   Grr!Grr!

James Carter

Derek the Dragon's Recipe for Damsel Pie

ONE DAMSEL
(dead or not, they taste great)

PASTRY
(you don't have to bother
with this to be honest)

COOKING INSTRUCTIONS . . .

Breathe over the damsel until nicely
crisp,
then scoff in one go!

James Carter

TheAncientGreeks . . .

TheAncientGreeks . . .
knew a thing
   or two
      about m o n s t e r s.

From their minds
   their mouths
      their myths
came c r e a t u r e s
   that still haunt us
      taunt us
         today.

Beware of the dog:
   the three-headed C e r b e r u s
      that guards the gates
         of the underworld.

Keep your eyes on the bull:
   with the body of a man
      he's as strong as he is tall
         the menacing M i n o t a u r.

It's rude to stare
   at M e d u s a
      with her snakes-for-hair
         one look alone
            will turn you to cold stone.

There's more besides
   and what's for sure
      they don't make b e a s t s
         like these any more.

James Carter

Unicorns

I stayed up all night, by the wood,
watching for a unicorn.

The horses came snorting from the misty
   field
to see what I was doing.

They pawed the ground
and shook their pearl manes,

their breath curled in the cold air
and their eyes reflected the moon.

After a while, they stood close,
warm and nodding gently,
to protect me.

Judith Green

The Dinosaur Rap

Come on, everybody, shake a claw.
Let's hear you bellow, let's hear you
    roar.
Let's hear you thump and clump and
    clap.
Come and join in. Do the dinosaur rap.

There's a young T-rex over by the door
Who's already stamped a hole in the
    floor.

There's a whirling, twirling apatosaurus
Encouraging everyone to join in the
    chorus.

Come on, everybody, shake a claw.
Let's hear you bellow, let's hear you
    roar.
Let's hear you thump and clump and
    clap.
Come and join in. Do the dinosaur rap. $\rightarrow$

There's a stegosaurus rattling his spines
And an iguanodon making thumbs-up
    signs.

There's an allosaurus giving a shout
As he thrashes and lashes his tail about.

Come on, everybody, shake a claw.
Let's hear you bellow. Let's hear you
    roar.
Let's hear you thump and clump and
    clap.
Come and join in. Do the dinosaur rap.

There's a triceratops who can't stop
    giggling
At the way her partner's writhing and
    wriggling.

There's an ankylosaurus swaying to the
    beat,
Clomping and clumping and stomping
    his feet.

There are dinosaurs here. There are
   dinosaurs there.
There are dinosaurs dancing
   everywhere.
So swing your tails and shake your
   claws.
Join in the rapping with the dinosaurs.

John Foster

Cloud Dragon

There's a dragon in the clouds:
Can't you see his open jaws?
And the spikes along his back?
And his twisty, crooked claws?
Look, he's changing shape now –
He's wider, not so tall:
Trying to fool us into thinking
He isn't there at all.
But be patient for a moment,
Just keep looking at the sky
And among the misty billows
That cloud dragon will come by.

Eric Finney

NATURE

Nature Table

I love the autumn table best
With crinkly leaves that curl to flame,
Acorns topped with fairy caps
And pumpkin huge as harvest moon.

I love the pine-cone Christmas trees,
The smooth, bright beads of hip and
   haw,
A chestnut's kindly, cow-eyed stare
The smell of winter in the making.

Karen Costello-McFeat

N is for Nature

N is for nature, a mother to all.

A is for animals, all great and small.

T is for tornadoes that tear up the land.

U is for underground, soil and sand.

R is for rainbows that never last long.

E is for Earth, the place we belong.

Angie Turner

What do you do on a Nature Walk?

We have an adventure, that's what –
crunching through the undergrowth,
dodging thorns and stings,
leaping logs and bridging bogs,
looking out for things:
birds and frogs and shy hedgehogs
and flies with fairy wings,
and slimy slugs and tiny bugs –
whatever nature brings!

Kate Williams

What we found at the seaside

Waves purring
wind stirring
    gulls chuckling
    crabs scuttling
spray splashing
fish dashing
    shells shimmering
    pebbles glimmering
pools gleaming
weeds steaming
    rocks crumbling
    stones tumbling
sand sliding
      sliding
        with the tide

Kate Williams

The Seven Ages of a Leaf

First the bud, close hugged,
Curled against the cold,
Waiting for sun's signal.

Then the newborn leaf,
Wrinkled, pale and fragile,
Freshly unfurling.

Then the growing leaf,
Full-veined, drinking deep,
Stretching, swelling, reaching.

Then the sun-baked leaf,
Spread wide, feeding upon light,
Working to store food for seed-making.

Then the celebration,
Garlanded in red and gold,
Richly signalling a job well done.

Sixth the fading leaf,
Withered and wrinkled,
Drifting down towards the waiting
    earth.

And then the seventh age,
Weakened and worm-eaten,
Journeying through the earth and roots
    and shoots

To reach the bud, close hugged,
Curled against the cold,
Waiting for sun's signal.

Julia Rawlinson

River

Whooshing

gushing

rushing

over

rocks.

Gabbling

babbling

scrabbling

over stones.

This way

that way

swaying under swans.

Slowing growing flowing to the sea.

Philip Waddell

The Apple

I hold an apple in my hand
And take a bite.
Inside it's crunchy, sweet and white.
I eat some more and more,
Till all that's left is the core
And inside *that* are pips,
Small and smooth and brown.
I'll take a single pip
And plant it in the ground
And watch it as it grows and grows,
Fed by rain and light,
Till, eventually, an apple tree is there,
Roots in the deep, dark soil,
Branches in the air
And full of juicy apples.
I'll pick one, hold it in my hand
And take a bite . . .

Gillian Floyd

Old Macdonald Had
Five Vowels, AEIOU
(A Lipogram Song!)

Old Macdonald had five vowels,
  A E I O U
And when she came across an a,
  this is what she'd do

Stack barn sacks
slap backs, pat cats, track bats
Stand slack and haphazard
Act awkward
walk backward

Old Macdonald had five vowels, aeiou
And when she came across an e, this is
  what she'd do

Get helpers, mend fences
(wretched senseless expenses!)
wet her knees, strew seeds
then fetch fresh cheeses –
spell-bent trees
meet the sweet bee breezes

Old MacDonald had five vowels, aeiou
And when she came across an *i*, this is
  what she'd do

Lift pigs, sift grits
Spit pits, fix bricks
Trim twigs, split sticks
Flick ticks in ricks

Old MacDonald had five vowels, aeiou
And when she came across an *o*, this is
  what she'd do

Bolt doors – stop hogs
cross cows, prod dogs
Chow down on corn –
Go forth – mow crops
Mop hog slops – go to town, to shops
flood ponds, plop rocks –
look now too how bold frog hops –
how crows swoop down off old
  rooftops

Old Macdonald had five vowels, aeiou,
And when she came across a *u*, this is
  what she'd do

→

Pluck ducks, pull bulls
Scrunch bugs
Slurp lunch
Tug mud-stuck trucks –
Trucks lurch!
Ugh! Crunch . .

Old Macdonald had five vowels, aeiou.

JonArno Lawson

Follow Me

Follow me, follow me
Under the alder tree
Down to the bank where the sleek
otters play,
Emperor dragonfly
Kingfisher flashing by
Blue, green and gold of a midsummer
day.

Follow me, follow me
By the bare alder tree
Bittersweet berries splash red on the snow,
Mirror carp, pike and bream
Held in an icy dream
Watching pale shadows from darkness
below.

Petonelle Archer

If I Close My Eyes

If I close my eyes
And sit under my tree,
When the wind blows
Through its leaves,
I can hear the sea.

If I close my eyes
And sit under my tree,
When the wind blows
Through its leaves,
And boughs and branches
Start to creak,
I'm sailing on the sea.

If I close my eyes
And sit under my tree.
When the wind blows
Through its leaves,
And boughs and branches
Start to creak
And sunlight dazzles
Like flashes of lightning
When I blink a peek,
I'm caught in a storm at sea.

But when the wind drops
Away from the leaves,
And boughs and branches
Spread silently,
I open my eyes very slowly,
Look up at the clouds
That drift above me,
I imagine fog-covered islands
And an undiscovered sea.

Kevin McCann

November Poem

Today is a grey day

A very grey day

Through the classroom window
I see grey walls,
grey roofs,
a grey fence

empty playground

Dull clouds smudge the sky.
There will be rain.
And the tired old tree is sulking,
leaves flown,
bare branches hanging.

Then comes the robin,
its signal flashing:
don't be worried

Christmas is coming.

"Stop staring out of the window, Amy,"
says Mrs Steel. "There's nothing to see."

I pick up my pencil

And keep one eye on the robin.

Danielle Sensier

PEOPLE WHO
HELP US

A Policeman Came to School

A policeman came to school today.
   This is what he had to say:

Keep away from railways,
   Don't play on the road,
Never talk to strangers
   or people you don't know.

Take a friend with you
   if you're playing in the park.
Tell Mum where you're going
   and be home before it's dark.

That's what the policeman had to say
   when he came to school today.

Celia Warren

Oh, Oh, the Story Man

Oh, oh, the story man
is opening the book.
He's holding up the pictures
so all of us can look.
He whispers all the quiet words
and yells the really loud ones.
Sometimes he drip-drops rainy words,
sometimes he swishes cloud ones.
When he reads about a snail
his voice slides slow and creepy,
when he reads about a bedtime bear
he yawns and sounds so sleepy.
I like the dragon story,
he reads it with a roar . . .
Down in the story corner
we all shout, "MORE!"

Jan Dean

School Librarian

Story time first, then she helps us
Choose a book to take
Home,
Offers good advice.
Our school
Librarian

Loves
Inspiring
Budding
Readers,
Asks us what we'd
Recommend and
Introduces real live
Authors, never says
"Not now, I'm busy."

Sue Cowling

Blue Flashing Light

On the top of an ambulance
A blue flashing light
Travels like a shooting star
Fast through the night.

Here is an emergency,
Somewhere someone's ill,
The blue star is rushing
While the night stands still.

Celia Warren

Dentist

She counts my teeth –
every single one in my pink gums
in case a sneaky one has just popped
   up
when nobody was looking.

She puts a mirror in my mouth
round and shiny as a 10p piece
then peeps in the between bits
in case I've missed a spot
when I've been cleaning.

She keeps my teeth
all gleamy white – so bright
I sometimes think
they could be beacons in the night.

Jan Dean

Lollipopped

The queen asked her driver,
"Why have we stopped?"
and the driver said, "Ma'am,
we have been lollipopped."

Mrs Jones asked her husband,
"George, why have we stopped?"
"I can't help it," said George,
"we have been lollipopped."

Passengers yelled,
"Hey, why have we stopped?"
and their bus driver shouted,
"We've been lollipopped."

The lollipop lady said,
"It's quite true.
If you drive to my crossing,
I'll lollipop you."

And the children all crossed
when the traffic had stopped
and waved at the cars
that had been lollipopped.

Marian Swinger

Santa in Zooland

When Santa went to Zooland
there were presents all around:
prezzies for the flyers
and those upon the ground.

The fish had scrummy fishcakes,
the dolphin had a bath,
the foxes had some foxgloves,
the hyenas had a laugh.

The camel had a bucket,
the sandflies all had spades,
the elephants had trumpets,
the bears some marmalade.

The polar bears had ice cream,
the pythons had a pie,
the crocodiles had toothpaste,
the dodo had a fly.

The owl had brand-new glasses,
the walrus had some skis,
the hedgehog had some cat food
(and powder for its fleas).

The tortoise had new rollerblades,
the turtle had some soup,
the chicken had an egg cup
and the penguin had a suit.

The mice were very happy –
they gave him one big squeak . . .
and asked him very nicely
to try to call each week.

Peter Dixon

The Hairdresser's Questions

"So, tell me,
do you want it crimped,
or do you want it curled?
Do you want it styled or wild,
or do you want it twirled?
Do you want a 'Grizzly Bear'?
    Tell me,
        tell me,
            tell me
                tell me,
how *do* you want your hair?"

"*Er . . . er . . .*"

"So, tell me,
do you want it gelled,
or do you want it fringed?
Do you want it fluffed or roughed,
or do you want it singed?
Do you want a 'Hedgehog Scare'?
    Tell me,
        tell me,
            tell me,
                tell me,
how *do* you want your hair?"

"*Er . . . er . . .*"

Wes Magee

Dinner Lady

Batter stirrer,
Egg-white whirrer,
Cabbage slicer,
Carrot dicer,
Gravy maker,
Pepper shaker,
Sausage fryer,
Shepherd's pie-er,
Apple corer,
Custard pourer,
Need-a-cuppa-
Washer-upper!

Sue Cowling

Excuse Me, Mrs Armitage, Can We Have Your Snow?

We're building a snow nose –
A giant white hooter,
A stonking great shnozzer
A real rooten-tooter.
But we've used all the snow
That fell in our yard.
And the stuff out the back
Is all crunchy and hard.
We want our snow nose
To be mega-tremendous
King Conk – Supersnout
El Nozolo Stupendous.
Please, Mrs Armitage,
Don't just say no.
Please Mrs Armitage
Don't tell us to go.
P l e a s e, Mrs Armitage,
Give us your snow!

Jan Dean

PETS

Jerri the Gerbil's Workout Programme

Beginners:

Round and round the wheel
Round and round the wheel

Intermediate:

Round and round the wheel
Round and round the wheel
Round and round the wheel
Round and round and round the wheel

Competent:

Round and round the wheel
Round and round the wheel
Round and round the wheel
Round and round and round the wheel
Up the stairs
Down the stairs
Round and round the wheel

Advanced:

Round and round the wheel
Round and round the wheel
Round and round the wheel
Round and round and round the wheel
Up the stairs
Down the stairs
Up the stairs
Down the stairs
In the plastic tube
1 – 2 – 3 – 4 –
Through the plastic tub
Up the stairs
Down the stairs
Round and round the wheel

Paul Cookson

I Did Not Eat the Goldfish

I did not eat the goldfish
It really was not me
At the time of the crime
I was sitting in a tree

I did not eat the goldfish
That's no word of a lie
I loved his silvery fins
And his mischievous eye

I did not eat the goldfish
I did not touch one golden scale
And I've no idea why pond weed
Is hanging from my tail

Roger Stevens

The Dizzy Hamster

Tell me, little hamster, how does it feel
Going round and round in your own
   little wheel?

Well, *said the hamster*, what I've found
Is when the wheel stops, then the room
   goes round.

Celia Warren

The Prayer of the Rabbits

Hail human, full of treats
water is with you.
Blessed are you among rabbit mothers
and blessed is your warm hand
when you stroke us. We like it when you
    croon
soft songs to us.
Take us not to the vets with her sharp
    needles
but bring us hay forever and ever.
Amen.

Angela Topping

I Like the Way You Hop, Rabbit

I like the way you hop, rabbit,
and the wobble flop of your lopsided
    ears
like the long silky petals
of a very furry daisy.
I like the way you nibble, rabbit,
all wrinkle-nosed and tippy toothed
as if the whole world was carrots
and nothing else mattered but the
    crunch.
I like the way you feel, rabbit,
velvet and hot-water-bottle cosy
and I love your round brown eyes.
Oh, rabbit, you are so beautiful to
    touch
I love everything about you
(except cleaning out your hutch).

                              Jan Dean

Puzzle the Puppy

Gina Douthwaite

New Dog Special Dog

I have a new dog, a special dog.
She says miaow and purrs,
rubs her black fur
against my leg.

I put her lead on
and take her for walks
but she prefers
to sit

at the bottom of a tree,
stare up at the birds
and listen, her tail twitching.
If she could fly, she would.

When I throw a stick for her
she looks the other way.
She has a mind of her own,
like me.

I'm proud of her.
How many dogs are there
who would like to fly?
I've always wanted a dog.

Cliff Yates

Cat's Eyes

Cat's eyes
grow wide
watching sparrows
eating scraps
of bread and bacon.

She sits on
the kitchen windowsill.

Unaware of her
they eat their fill
and fly
away.

Cat yawns.
Cat sighs.

Cat's eyes
close

(almost).

Bernard Young

Kitten

I pounce
and bounce

and creep
and leap.

I twitch
and itch

and scratch
and snatch.

I play
all day

then arch
and stretch

and sleep.

Jill Townsend

What Am I?

Leg-brusher,
Mouse-trapper.
Flea-houser
Milk-lapper.

Night-stalker,
Purr-maker.
Fur-licker,
Cheese-taker.

Day-sleeper,
Fly-catcher.
Mini-tiger,
Bird-snatcher.

Pie Corbett

(A cat)

PIRATES

How to Be a Pirate

First you need a hat
One with three corners or perhaps
One like Nelson wears on his column
But add a skull and crossbones.

Failing that, make one out of paper.

Then you will need a coat
A big, green, velvet number
With huge cuffs and gold buttons.

Failing that, an old trackie top will do.

Get some sea boots
Long and leathery, soaked
In salt and the blood of your enemy.

Failing that, try some wellies.

Of course you'll need a parrot
Perched on your shoulder
One that squawks and shouts
"Pieces of eight, pieces of eight"

Failing that, get a wooden one
At the toyshop.

You need a cutlass
A pistol, some knives
And a blunderbuss
Buy them at the Pirate Store.

Failing that, go back to the toyshop.

Then you'll have to find a map
Of Broken-Skull Island
In some old tea chest
There's swamps and skeletons
And X marks the spot

Failing that, draw one in crayon
On some old rolls of wallpaper.

Now you'll need a ship
Three masts full of sail
Three decks full of cannons. $\longrightarrow$

Failing that, try a tree
Leafy rigging and ropes of sunlight
Or an old table, upside down
With mops as masts.

Set sail at once
Dig up your treasure
Even it does look a bit
Like Dad's daffodil bulbs
And a handful of papers.

Failing that, go to the sweet shop
For some chocolate money

Then practise
Saying "Yo-ho-ho
Shiver me timbers, I'll slice
Yer gizzards, you scurvy landlubber."

Failing that, go inside for some tea.

David Harmer

Shiver Me Timbers!
Yo-Ho-Ho!

Shiver me timbers! Yo-ho-ho!
Arrr, arrr, arrr, me hearty!
Son of a gun, there's a tot of rum,
If you sail with our pirate party.

Don't hesitate or you'll be too late,
For we sail on the evening tide.
There's no time to lose, so be quick and
    choose.
Climb aboard or step aside.

Forget about home, there's a world to
    roam.
Take a last look at the land.
Join our crew and we'll make a man of
    you,
When you're one of our pirate band.

Shiver me timbers! Yo-ho-ho!
Arrr, arrr, arrr, me hearty.
There's a swig of grog, you scurvy dog!
When you join our pirate party.

John Foster

Speaking Pirate

I be a pirate, that I be.
I speaks very pir-at-i-cally.
You can be a pirate and join the crew,
But you must speak like a pirate do!

Just shout Ahoy!
AHOY!
Shout Avast
AVAST!
Swab the decks and dance a jig,
Nail your colours to the mast!

I be a pirate, that I be.
I speaks very piratically.
Come this way and join the crew,
Then you can speak like a pirate too!

Shout Oo-arr!
OO-ARRRRR!
Shout Yo-ho!
YO-HO!
Walk the plank and dance a jig.
Across the seas we go!

I be a pirate, that I be.
I speaks very piratically.
I be a pirate, you've joined the crew.
Now you speak like a pirate too!
AHOY!

Michaela Morgan

Amelia the Pirate

I
catch
the scent,
of briny breath,
I gaze upon the blue;
as once did Captain Black-
beard with his famous pirate
crew. One day I'll sail the ocean's
depths and travel far abroad. The world
will dread "Amelia, the fearless Pirate Lord!"
I'll
rob
the Spanish galleons and seize their chests of gold. I'll make their
captains walk the plank, just like in days of old. A pirate's life's
the life for me, there's only one small catch: I think I'll have
to lose an eye and wear a pirate's patch! I'd also need a
wooden leg, gold teeth, an iron hook! Perhaps I'll stay
at home instead and read a pirate book!

Paul Hughes

Pirates

Pirates dress in red and gold
They sail on a sea of blue
Their ship is brown
The sails are white
The flag is black,
As black as night,
Did you ever see such a colourful sight
As the jolly pirate crew?

Roger Stevens

12 Ways to Spot a Pirate in Disguise

1. A peg leg peeping
   From the bottom of his jeans

2. He might look like your head teacher
   He might shout like your head teacher
   He might dress like your head teacher
   But he still says "Ah-harrrrrr"
   And calls you "Jim lad."

3. Who are all those people
   Covered in long coats
   Waiting outside the pet shop
   Under a sign saying "Cut-Price Parrots!"

4. Some people have a car on the drive
   Some people have a caravan on the
   drive
   But not many people
   Have a three-masted sloop with
   cannons
   On the drive.

5. Most policemen
   Don't wear a three-cornered hat with
   a feather
   Instead of a helmet.

6. You've got an England football flag
   In your window. Next door
   They've got a Jolly Roger.

7. Is there a house on your street
   Called "Dunpirating"?

8. On the shelves
   In the school library
   Are there only copies
   Of *Treasure Island*?

9. When you buy some sweets
   At the corner shop
   Do you get your change
   In pieces of eight? →

10. Is the postman
    Wearing a long cutlass
    As well as his postbag?

11. Does the lollipop lady
    Leave you marooned
    On a traffic island?

12. Look hard at your teacher
    Does he or she have
    A large tattoo saying
    "I loves to be a pirate"?

David Harmer

Pirate

I'm a pirate with a parrot on my
    shoulder.
I'm a pirate with a cutlass in my hand.
I sail upon the briny
With a hat that's black and shiny
And a pistol that's particularly grand.

As a pet a parrot's perfect for a pirate,
So much better than a hamster or a
    hen.
We get pleasure beyond measure
Digging up a chest of treasure,
And afterwards we bury it again.

John Whitworth

It's a Pirate's Life for Me

Pull up the anchor with a Yo-heave-ho!
Set a course for the open sea.
Never mind what I'm leaving behind,
It's a pirate's life for me.

Hoist up the mainsail with a Yo-heave-
    ho!
Ride with the tide, as we go
With never a care and the wind in our
    hair,
It's a pirate's life for me.

Sitting in the crow's nest, high above
    the waves,
Sight a ship on the starboard bow.
In the dead of night, get ready for a
    fight.
It's a pirate's life for me.

Fire a broadside as we pull alongside,
Then jump aboard from a rope.
On the deck we stand, fighting hand to
    hand.
It's a pirate's life for me.

In just quarter of an hour we overpower
The captain of the ship and his crew.
Then we climb into the hold to search
    for gold.
It's a pirate's life for me.

There are thirty chests or more, full of
    jewels galore,
Which sparkle and gleam in the dark.
So we take the ship in tow and off we
    go.
It's a pirate's life for me.

We sail to a lonely isle, and stop for a
    while
To bury the chests on the shore.
On a map we mark where we buried
    them there.
It's a pirate's life for me.

Pull up the anchor with a Yo-heave-ho!
Set a course for the open sea.
Never mind what I left behind.
It's a pirate's life for me.

John Foster

Boring Mr Grimble

Creeping past the gym last night
I heard a chilling cry –
And there was Mr Grimble
(Boring Mr Grimble
With the neatly knotted tie),
Swinging from the wall bars
With a patch across his eye.

He raised the skull and crossbones
While the floor rocked to and fro,
And I hid from Mr Grimble
(Boring Mr Grimble
With his voice so soft and low),
When his silver earring glinted
And he thundered, "Yo-ho-ho!"

Sitting in my class today
I squeeze my eyelids tight,
And I still see Mr Grimble
(Boring Mr Grimble
With his shoes so shiny bright),
Brandishing his cutlass
As our school sails through the night.

Clare Bevan

The Pirates Are Walking the Plank

The pirates are walking the plank,
the pirates are walking the plank.
At the old Dogger Bank
where it's wet and it's dank
the pirates are walking the plank.
SPER-LASH!

Those peg-legged,
patch-eyed,
pig-tailed,
hair-dyed
pirates
are walking the plank today.
HEY!

Those big-nosed,
bristle-chinned,
earringed,
wide-grinned
pirates
are walking the plank today.
HEY!

The pirates are walking the plank,
the pirates are walking the plank.
At the old Dogger Bank
where it's wet and it's dank
the pirates are walking the plank.
SPER-LASH!

Wes Magee

A Letter Home

Dear Ma and Pa,
       The food is bad, the sea is
rough, the captain is grumpy and the
boatswain's tough. I'm cramped in
my hammock, my britches are tight,
I've got no dry clothes and it's freezing
at night. I came in search of riches,
of caskets full of gold, but all I've
managed to pick up is scurvy and a
cold.
  I don't think much of fighting and
rigging sails is tough. A pirate's life is not
for me, I think I've had enough.
    Anyway I'd better go, I've got to
scrub the deck, and if the captain finds
me here he'll wring my scrawny neck.

Your loving son,
Nathaniel Hawkins

Richard Caley

SEASONS AND
WEATHER

On a Wild, Wild Walk...

On a wild, wild walk
a while ago

*We climbed a hill
we turned a bend
we crossed a stream
we stopped and then . . . SNOW!*

Big snow thick snow
snow you could lick snow
white snow bright snow
snow snow snow!

CHORUS: *We climbed . . . WIND!*

Big wind warm wind
blowing up a storm wind
high wind wild wind
wind wind wind!

CHORUS: *We climbed . . . RAIN!*

Big rain wet rain
hard as you can get rain
warm rain storm rain
rain rain rain!

CHORUS: *We climbed . . . MIST!*

Big mist white mist
oh what a sight mist
high mist wide mist
mist mist mist!

CHORUS: *We climbed . . . SUN!*

Big sun hot sun
oh what a lot sun
bright sun light sun
sun sun sun!

It all began with a fall of snow –
on a wild, wild walk
a while ago

James Carter

Autumn, Winter, Spring, Summer

Katie stood under a tree.
It was autumn and she was five.
In the still air one little leaf drifted
Then came to rest, red on her yellow
  hair
As if it was a butterfly.

Katie stood under a tree.
It was winter. The branches were
  empty.
She looked up and saw every bend in
  the twigs
Like an ink drawing on the clear white
  sky
And small birds swooping and diving.

Katie stood under a tree.
It was spring and all the twigs and
  branches
Were thickened and crowded with the
  light green leaves
That moved against the sky, but didn't
  blow off
To fly with the flocks of birds, wheeling
  and landing.

Katie stood under a tree.
It was summer and she was six.
The tree was full and a thick rustling
  canopy
Made a shelter of shade so the sun did
  not burn her.
The tree was quite full and complete
And Katie was six.

Jenny Joseph

Run to the Hilltop

Run to the hilltop,
Race to the sea,
Fly across the cornfields –
You can't catch me.

When autumn calls
    I blow the leaves.
When winter creeps
    I make you sneeze.

      Run to the hilltop,
      Race to the sea,
      Fly across the cornfields –
      You can't catch me.

In summer I chase the clouds away
So you can have a sunny day.

I tickle blossoms in the spring
Till they bloom bright and make you
    sing.

Run to the hilltop,
Race to the sea –
I AM THE WIND
And you can't catch me.

David Greygoose

Trudging through the Snow

I
  love
    trudging
      through
        the
            snow
          leaving
        behind
          footsteps
        like
    a
      row
    of
  buttonholes
  in
a
  white
    sweater.
    I
love
  the
      crunchy
        sound
      my
  boots
make
  as

174

I
    weave
        zigzag
            patterns
                on
            untrodden
        ground.
    I
love
    drawing
        in
            the
        snow,
    making
angel
shapes
with
    my
        outstretched
            arms.
            I
    love
being
first
    into
        this
            magic
                world.

    Moira Andrew

Hush Now

The thing about snow is
It makes everything quiet –
Except, of course, for children
Snow just makes them riot.

Mike Barfield

Summer Picture

A blue boat
dances
across glass-green waves,
its white sails
fluttering
like butterflies.

Moira Andrew

Rainbow

Rainbow arching in the sky
How your colours glow
Red, Orange, Yellow, Green
Blue and Indigo.

Violet sits there underneath
Glad to take the strain
Of the bridge which always comes to
  life
When sunshine follows rain.

Richard Caley

Look

The tree is wearing cherries
dotted like rubies in its emerald hair.
Here and here,
there and there,
red cherries glistening in the leafy green
    air.

Jan Dean

Haiku Nightlight

On midsummer nights
Fireflies melt holes in the dark
Letting the light through.

Judith Green

A Complaint

I can
land lightly on leaves
in soft plump
drops

I can
fall in fevered fists
pounding out the oldest
beat of all

I can
coax flowered flares
of life from
a dusty little seed

I can
bend mighty rays of sunlight
to paint the sky
with a rainbow

and what thanks do I get for
my artistry?

a roll of the eyes
a tight-lipped tut
and the tug of a hood

Matt Goodfellow

Fallen Leaves

After the dancing of May,
After the long summer days,
When autumn comes
     and the laughter is gone,
Then we are just fallen leaves.

David Greygoose

Autumn Fields

Mists at morning
swirled aside
by frost-edged winds,
to let a lemon sun
cast purple shadows
on to fields
of freshly fallen leaves
waiting for winter wheat
to help them hide
the frozen furrows'
barren brown.

Brian Davies

Autumnfall

                    leaf
       leaf   leaf
                    leaf
         leaf   leaf
                    leaf
             leaf   leaf
       leaf
                    leaf
          leaf   leaf
                    leaf
                    leaf
           leaf   leaf   leaf
       leafleafleafleafleafleafleaf
      leafleafleafleafleafleafleafleatleaf
     leafleafleafleafleafleafleafleatleafleaf
    leafleafleafleaf**HEDGEHOG**leafleafleafleaf

                                Mike Johnson

184

SENSES

The Sound of Music

The singing of the violin
Is like a spiky silver pin.

The whisper of the sideways flute
Slips and slithers like a newt.

The growling of the double bass
Prowls around a gloomy place.

The clatter of the xylophones
Rattles like a box of bones.

The grand piano wistfully
Ripples like a moonlit sea.

The oboe echoes round the hall,
Mournful as a mermaid's call.

But drums are like a firework night,
Setting all my thoughts alight.

Clare Bevan

Music ...

is everywhere.
In the birds of the air.
In the hum of the honeybee.
In the song of the breeze
rustling the trees.
In the river that murmurs
over the stones.
In the snow wind that moans.

In the surge of the sea
lapping the shore.
In the roar of the wind
rattling the door.
The rumble of thunder
and drum of the rain
on the windowpane.
Music is here.
Filling your ear.

Ann Bonner

HELLO!

"HELLO!" I shouted in a jar,
then screwed the lid on tight.
I thought my shout
could not get out,
and left it overnight.

Alas, the jar was empty
when I opened it today.
I held it near,
but couldn't hear "HELLO!"
It's got away!

So anywhere you're wandering,
or even out at sea,
if you should hear a friendly shout
when no one seems to be about,
it might have come from me.

Barry Buckingham

Flashy

Ian Larmont

Pleasant Scents

The kitchen just before lunch on
    Christmas Day . . .
Salty spray when waves crash on rocks
    in the bay . . .
In school, when you model with
    clammy damp clay . . .
        Pleasant scents
        that stay with you
            forever.

The attic's dry air after days of June
    heat . . .
A shower of spring rain that refreshes
    the street . . .
An orange you peel: the tang sharp,
    yet so sweet . . .
        Pleasant scents
        that stay with you
            forever.

The Bonfire Night smoke as it drifts in the
   dark . . .
Air lemony-clean on the Island of
   Sark . . .
Mint in the back garden . . . and mud in
   the park . . .
       Pleasant scents
       that stay with you
          forever.

Wes Magee

Sounds

I like to hear
snakes hissing in the wind,
a ball hitting a bat,
sea crashing on the shore,
rain patting on my window,
a monster chewing someone's bones,
dogs barking, water dripping,
and my cat mew for more.

I like to hear
the sound of bees buzzing,
and a record jumping,
the dead leaves crunching,
and the last bell at school.

I like to hear
the sound of a dinosaur's foot,
no sound at all,
clocks tick-tocking,
Rice Krispies popping,
the munching of sweets.

I like to hear
the sound of cheeks puffing,
children shouting,
a heartbeat beating,
warm clothes rustling,
the sound of me and you

Robin Mellor

Sounds of School

Listen up!
Listen in!
Are you REALLY listening?
What do you hear?

The shriekings in the playground,
The creaking of a door,
The sound of feet pattering, down the
    corridor.

The thumping of a football.
The cries and shouts of SCORE!!
The clinking of the coffee cups behind
    the staffroom door.

Faint music from assembly,
The quiet march of feet.
The shufflings of bottoms, that need a
    comfy seat?

The rustling of the paper,
The whisper of a page,
The scritch and scratchy scufflings of
    our hamster in his cage?

The murmurings and mutterings,
chit-chatter and a sigh.
The rush of traffic outside in the
    distance zooming by?

Ticks and clicks and clattering
A slam, a squeak, a cheer.
Are you really listening
What do you hear?

Michaela Morgan

Files Not Found on a Computer

The Touch File

a son stroking his father's cheek,
fingers folding a hamster's fur,
a face buried in cherry blossom,
enclosing arms of goodnight.

The Taste File

the saltiness of boiled ham
against soft white bread,
the sharpness of marmalade
melding with butter on wholemeal
   toast,
the twang of rhubarb and ginger
hiding beneath crunchy crumble,
the cut of iced sparkling water
swilling down my throat.

The Aroma File

a wet dog in the rain,
garlic squashed beneath a knife,
lavender steaming from my bath,
croissant warming Sunday morning.

Chrissie Gittins

Sniff, Sniff . . .

My school smells of . . .
Plimsolls and pencils,
And pasta for lunch.

My teacher smells of . . .
Coffee and classrooms
And cough drops to crunch.

My friend smells of . . .
Playgrounds and popcorn
And peppermint sweets.

My dog smells of . . .
Baskets and biscuits
And bone-flavoured treats.

My gran smells of . . .
Crumpets and cocoa
And cakes freshly baked.

My dad smells of . . .
Gardens and grasses
And ground neatly raked.

My sister smells of . . .
Nose-numbing perfume
And nail varnish (bright!)

My mum smells of . . .
Talcum and toast when
She tucks me up tight.

Clare Bevan

What a Peach

I love you, my darling, my dear.
Your honey skin is soft and clear.
Your scent is heaven to my nose –
You're far more lovely than a rose.
Your flesh is firm and sweet and good –
But, oh, your heart is made of wood.

Angela Topping

A Sense of Weather

I love the sound of rain
splishing and splashing
in grey-gurgly gutters.

I love the feel of sunshine
blazing and blistering
on hazy summer days.

I love the taste of snow
melting and mingling
on the tip of my tongue.

I love the look of rainbows
glittering and glistening
across a sun-stormy sky.

I love the smell of frost
frizzling and frazzling
on ice-sparkly mornings.

Moira Andrew

Weather Sense

See the lightning
    Split the sky.

Hear the thunder
    Rumbling by.

Feel the wind
    Bringing rain.

Smell the world
Washed clean again.

And now it's clear
The storm is done –

Taste a strawberry
    Warmed by sun.

Eric Finney

SCHOOL

Show and Tell

Amber showed a little shell
Bella told us how she fell
Carla went to see her nan
Daniel went to see West Ham
Ella did a ballet dance
Faron's daddy went to France
Georgia talked about her auntie
Hannah's going to have a party
Ian brought his football cards
Joey showed his model cars
Kieran told us he'd been naughty
Lauren counted up to forty
Maddie sang her favourite song
Noah's baby won't be long
Ollie went to Daniel's home
Paris had an ice-cream cone
Quentin showed a paper swan
Rohan's brother's nearly one
Sarah made a frog with clay
Tina's nana came to stay
Usha's learning how to swim
Vinny brought some acorns in
Winston laughed and told a joke

Ma**X** put on his wizard's cloak
Yasmine said a funny rhyme
Zoe said she'd show next time

James Carter

Our Headmaster

He ruffles your hair when you go by,
knows your name. He can sort out
any mess from sewing to sums.
He's like Superman, he can fly.
He is calm with those who shout.
He's shy of grown-up dads and mums.

Angela Topping

I Can...

Count to a hundred,
Read and write,
Draw a picture,
Fly a kite,
Rollerblade
Do a handstand,
Play a tune
With an elastic band,
Swim a length,
Multiply,
Kick a football
Play I Spy,
Use a computer,
Tie my shoe,
I can do
Lots of things
– what about you?

Tony Langham

L is for Library

Don't be fooled!

A library may LOOK like a room,
But really, it is a magical street
Lined with many-coloured doors.

Walk through this one,
And step back, back,
To faraway places
Where Romans march, or castles glitter,
Or small children skate
On a frozen river.

Open this one,
And enter the dark cage of a jungle
Where great black cats watch you
With golden eyes,
And emerald insects flit around your
    head
Like living jewels.

Try this one,
And massive machines will roar
And spit fire at you like story monsters,
While excited inventors amaze you
With their electronic tricks.

Or what about this door?
The one with the dragon-head handle?
Let it creak aside and welcome you
To endless Wonderlands.
Here are white rabbits, of course.
And sorrowful grey donkeys,
And wizards, and wild woods,
And stormy seas,
And stolen treasures,
And purple planets,
And talking mice,
And all the beasts that ever were,
Or NEVER were –
The unicorn, the phoenix,
And your very own flying horse.

Gallop away!
Explore all the doors,
Discover the wide world that is called
Imagination,
And you will not be fooled
By clever disguises.

A library only LOOKS like a room.

Clare Bevan

Colouring In

And staying inside the lines
Is fine, but . . .
I like it when stuff leaks –
When the blue bird and the blue sky
Are just one blur of blue blue flying,
And the feeling of the feathers in the air
And the wind along the blade of wing
Is a long gash of smudgy colour.
I like it when the flowers and the
  sunshine
Puddle red and yellow into orange,
The way the hot sun on my back
Lulls me – muddles me – sleepy
In the scented garden,
Makes me part of the picture . . .
Part of the place.

Jan Dean

Sitting-Still Time

After play
and sometimes before play
we practise
SITTING STILL.
I do not like sitting-still time.
I prefer wrestling, rolling and charging
    round with my friends time.
Our teacher says
that if we try our very hardest
we could
    would
    or might
WIN A SITTING-STILL GOLD MEDAL
But: I would rather
    win a gold medal
    for charging round
    the room
    with Scottie Wilson
    and Fred Sedgwick.

                    Yea!

                            Peter Dixon

Playtime

Playtime, out-time,
Never any doubt time
What it's all about time
When you need to shout time.

Playtime, free-time,
Hide behind the tree time
Miss, he's chasing me time
Fall and graze your knee time.

Playtime, fool-time,
Run back into school time
Act really cool time
Don't you know the rule time?

Playtime, wait-time,
Chat to your mate time
Hang around the gate time
Till you're nearly late time.

Playtime, in-time,
Put that in the bin time
What's that awful din? time
Get rid of that grin time.

Playtime, playtime,
Wish you could just stay time.

Michael Lockwood

Our Class's Hamster Horatio

Sometimes it's my turn
to take him to our house
for the weekend. We celebrate.
I give him the nicest titbits
and he spins and spins on his wheel.

When I take him out of his cage,
he wanders about my room.
He is extremely curious
and sniffs at everything in his path.
But I watch him constantly
in case he zooms away.

Katherine Gallagher

According to Our
Dinner Ladies...

We pour through the gates like cereal
   from a box
Full of Snap, Crackle and Pop.

In the corridors between classes
We chatter like cutlery clattering china.

Every playtime we chase around the
   playground
Like peas around a plate –

Which is why, by going-home time,
We're as limp as leftover lettuces.

Philip Waddell

Goodbye Rhyme

We're ready now
It's time to say
we've tidied up
and cleared away

We've done our work
been out to play
we've learned a lot
in just a day

We read a book
we talked, we sang
we did PE
we hopped, we ran

We looked for bugs
we caught a few
we watched them crawl
we drew them too

We're in our coats
and here we're sat
we're all together
on the mat

So now we've done
our goodbye rhyme
we'll all stand up
for homeward time!

James Carter

Home Time

Be at the gate.
Don't be late.
You will come,
won't you, Mum?

Jill Townsend

This Is Where...

... this is where I learnt to be.
And this is where I learnt to read,
and write and count and act in plays,
and blossom in so many ways.

This is where I learnt to sing,
express myself, and really think.
And this is where I learnt to dream,
to wonder why and what things mean.

This is where I learnt to care,
to make good friends, to give, to share,
to kick, to catch, to race, to run.
This is where I had such fun.

This is where I grew and grew.
This is where? My primary school!

James Carter

SPACE

Space

S tars
P lanets
A steroids
C onstellations
E xtraterrestrials

Celia Gentles

Space

Stuffed with stars
Packed with planets
Abundant in asteroids
Crammed with constellations
Endlessly expanding?

Philip Waddell

Footprints

There is a footprint
On the beach

There is a footprint
On the moon

There are no footprints
On Mars

But perhaps there will be
Soon

Roger Stevens

Winter Night

When it's daytime,
The frost glistens and glints
Like a galaxy of fallen stars.
When it's night-time,
The cold black sky
Shimmers and glimmers
As if it's freckled with freezing frost.

Tim Pointon

Alliteration Space-Station Countdown

10 purple planets
9 neon nights
8 rocking rockets
7 shooting stars
6 silver saucers
5 crazy comets
4 sparkling satellites
3 mighty meteorites
2 misty moons
1 shining sun

Paul Cookson

Gravity

If it wasn't for earth's
gravitational pull
then objects would float up
and skies would be full
of ripe conkers, bombs, cow-dung,
those pencils we lose
from coat pockets, high jumpers
like large kangaroos,
confetti, leaves, litter,
a melee of fruit,
all those sticks thrown for puppies
and the footballs we boot.
Imagine: this planet
a much tidier place.

But think of that mess up in space.

Rachel Rooney

black magic

when the night is black
and the moon
gloomily frays at its edges
crumple a rag of tattered cloud

flick away the cobwebs
wipe away the smears
polish until the moon is shiny
and the night is clear

shake out the rag
scattering moondust

discover stars

Lynne Taylor

Space Rocket

Super, shiny space rocket
Shoot me to the stars
Land me safely on the moon
Then carry me to Mars.

Fire me into orbit
Beyond the Milky Way
Then loop-the-loop through Saturn's
    rings
What fun we'll have today.

Take me to the planets
That no one else has seen
Like Jupiter with golden clouds
Or Pluto shining green.

Super, shiny space rocket
Please let me fly with you
Together we can cruise the sky
And make my dreams come true.

Richard Caley

Dark Sky Lullaby

Go to sleep, baby,
     little child of mine.
I love you as the planets speed
     and while the stars shine.

Go to sleep, baby,
     go to sleep soon.
I love you as the sun rolls,
     and at the tumbling of the moon.

John Rice

Twinkle, Twinkle

Twinkle, twinkle, not a star
But a satellite you are.
Up above the world so high,
Moving steadily through the sky.
Twinkle, twinkle, like a star,
telling motorists where they are.

Trevor Parsons

Cargoes

Pan-galactic trader from distant Orion
warping into hyperdrive off Antares
    Four
with a cargo of avorium,
and frazel and zignuts,
sandawoop, cedrawoop, and sweet
    white glor.

Stately interstellar ship coming from Tau
    Ceti
surging into lightspeed by Pavonian ice
with a cargo of plutionds,
zermerilds, argothysts,
kinjals, ballisets and arrakian spice.

Dirty Terran freighter with a clart-caked
    blast-tube
butting through the asteroid belt in the
    solar wind
with a cargo of chrondite,
stale stroon, polygunk,
fish-meat powder and baked beans
    (tinned).

Dave Calder

THE PAST

The Past

The past is full of cavemen dressed in
    animal skins,
Running around chasing mammoths,
Waving clubs above their heads.

And Roman emperors wearing togas,
Eating grapes and swans and dormice,
Wearing sandals while Vesuvius erupts.

And knights struggling into suits of
    armour,
Galloping about on horses, brandishing
    swords,
And living in draughty castles.

And Queen Elizabeth I,
Standing stiffly in so many clothes that
    she can hardly move,
While someone trills and strums to
    entertain her.

And bombs dropping from aeroplanes
Into jungles and seas of mud,
And cities where sirens are blaring.

And grannies and grandads,
Wearing old-fashioned coats and hats,
Driving to the seaside in cranky cars,
    with picnic hampers.

And Mum meeting Dad,
When Mum wasn't Mum and Dad
    wasn't Dad,
And I wasn't anything.

And playing football in the playground
    yesterday,
And the head teacher droning on in
    assembly,
And Mum cooking sausages for tea.

And writing the line before this,
And the line before this,
And the line before this . . .

Julia Rawlinson

Picture of Granny

Granny has a picture.
She says it is her mother,
and there's a little girl
standing with her brother.

"That's me when I was six
and Uncle Tom was four."
I've never thought of Granny
as a girl before.

Jill Townsend

New Year's Resolutions

1. Go to Hastings
2. Kill Harold
3. Beat Britain
4. Build castles
5. Don't forget wine

Signed *Norman the Conqueror, 1066*

Danielle Sensier

The Past Comes in Different Lengths

A goal-kick away
– the ball's sure route
from boot tip to net.

A birthday away
– a year unfolding from newborn
to puffing at one sugar-iced flame.

A family tree away
– a great-great-uncle's life from cabin
   boy
to silk top hat and stiff-suit photograph.

An aeon away
– wigglesome evolution from sea slug
to elegant yellow giraffe.

Far away,
    near away,
        a laugh away,
            a heartbeat.

Mandy Coe

What I Heard from the Castle Kitchen

The hoot of an owl
The howl of the wind
The rustle of mice
The drip of a well
The clop of a hoof
The roll of a stone
The boom of a knock
The creak of a door

The swish of a gown
The tramping of feet
The murmur of voices
The chill of a gasp
The clashing of swords
The bashing of shields
The clanking of chains
The king's mighty roar

Kate Williams

My Past

My Past is a box full of old ideas
My Past is a deep still lake
My Past can be a book of laughter or a
   bucket of tears
My Past hides chances I did not take

My Past is a trail of footprints
that never runs in front of me
My Past gets bigger and bigger
building a mountain of memories

My Past will be with me for all my years
Through days of sunshine, days of rain
My Past is something I hold dear
A path I will not walk again

Phil Rampton

My Old Bedroom

The room they gave me.
The room that was too small.
The room that there were rules about:
No posters, no drawing pins, no Blu-Tack.
The room I wrote my diary in
And dreamed of writing more than
   that.
The room that disappeared
When I stepped inside a storybook.
The room that I escaped from.

Anna Wilson

The Past

The past was yesterday, you know
The day before and once more
And so on forever.

Past my mum and dad and gran
Past her mum and dad and gran
Past her gran's gran's gran's gran's
    gran.

Like a road we walk along
And turn around to look behind
To see it stretch and stretch away.

Until it stops at the day
Where it started, long ago
And you can't go back any more.

When was that? I wonder.

                        David Harmer

Urgent

WANTED

Sturdy boy for castle kitchen.

No experience.

Full training will be given.

Must not mind strong smells,

sharp knives, heat, cold, rats,

long hours at the spit.

Live in. Own mattress necessary.

Ask for Head Cook (soon!)

Sue Cowling

The Great Fire

The summer's been a scorcher.
There's still no sign of rain.
A baker's left his oven on
Down in Pudding Lane!
So go and tell the king,
Wake the Lord Mayor from his bed.
The wind is from the east
Which means the fire is sure to spread.

Now London Bridge is burning,
Our houses all are gone,
The churches are in ruins,
Streets too hot to walk upon!
So go and fetch a bucket
And join the human chain
To fight the mighty blaze
That started down in Pudding Lane.

Sue Cowling

Remembrance

Red poppies at
Eleven in the
Morning on the
Eleventh day of the eleventh
Month. We
Bow our heads
Respectfully
And think of those who did
Not live to
Celebrate peace and the
End of fighting.

Sue Cowling

THE SEASIDE

My Favourite Holiday

I love swimming
in cold waves
under brilliant sun.

I run sand
through my fingers,
scrunch shells underfoot.

A crab scuttles.
Fish flash silver.
Wet pebbles sparkle.

Alison Chisholm

Hungry Wave

Take home your buckets,
Take home your seashells,
Take home your trousers rolled up to
 the knees,
Take home your surfboards,
Take home your suncream
But leave me some sandcastles, please!

Sue Cowling

At the Seaside

We'll have a splish time, a splash time
A watch-the-tall-waves-crash time,
At the seaside.

We'll have a salty-sandy-hand time
A hear-the-big-loud-band time,
At the seaside.

We'll have a slippery-seaweed-smell
   time
A find-a-shiny-shell time,
At the seaside.

And we'll have a wave-goodbye-to-
   the-bay time
A wish-that-we-could-stay time
A hip-hip-hip-hooray time,
For the seaside.

Coral Rumble

Through the Dark

"We'll drive through the dark," Dad said,
"And avoid the jams that way."
So we set out well before midnight
at the start of our holiday.

Above us the big black sky
with a glimpse of a star or two.
In front of us, long weary hours
with nothing much to do.

Mum thought she spotted a fox
as we skirted the edge of a town,
I'm sure that I saw a UFO
with its ray of light beaming down.

We stopped for something to eat
at a twenty-four-hour cafe,
then hour after hour passed by
on our dark strip of motorway.

Till Dad said, "It's really a shame,
you're missing a gorgeous sunrise."
But I was too tired to notice.
I just couldn't open my eyes.

Brian Moses

Holiday Scrap-Box

A dull white pebble
That misses the ocean
A Greek postage stamp
Of Aristotle's head
A strand of dried seaweed
Out of its depth
A fragile ball of sponge
Found on the seabed
A postcard of ruins
With a sizzling blue sky
A photograph of Grandad
With the dog with one eye

Roger Stevens

Shells and Stones

Shells and stones on my windowsill
All collected by me.
Shells and stones bring back memories
Of holidays by the sea.

I remember our sandcastle crumbling
As the tide crept up the beach
And white waves foaming and
    tumbling –
Where would the next one reach?

I remember peering in rock pools
And the cold, dark caves we explored
And looking down from the clifftops
Where the seagulls swung and soared.

Seashells and smooth pink stones
All collected by me:
Memories on my windowsill.
Let's go back to the sea!

Eric Finney

A Day at the Seaside

Sand on my face
Salt on my lips
Sand in my hair
Salt on my chips.

Jane Saddler

Holiday Swims

On Saltwick Nab
with teeth a-chatter
my father said
   it didn't matter
that northern seas
and icy breeze
should stab our flesh
and gnaw our knees.
   Cold does you good,
he would explain
in a lash of wind
and a flail of rain.
   It's really nice –
   come on in . . .
balding head,
icy grin.

In dripping costumes made by Mum,
we strugggle home from father's fun
and by warm fires
forget the pain
and ask that we might go again.

Peter Dixon

Tillynaught Junction

On this platform everything changed
after the long journey in the stuffy
carriage
to walk from one side of this platform to
the other
dragging strapped cases, and stand
there, tired and sticky,
was to feel an invisible frontier had
been crossed
and the connection to school and city
had steamed away
and we were left here among a sea of
fields
with the birdsong and sometimes a
shuffling cow
with the shadow of the signal and the
empty waiting room –
and no one ever seemed to be waiting
for in between trains it was a place
without time
and I would wander the platform edge
looking at weeds, the single track, the
signal box,

the curve of line that I knew led like a
   lane
through the hidden folds of the farmed
   land
to its horizon with the huge sky and
   suddenly
the sea, the familiar rocks, beaches,
   links –
the real arrival on holiday

and yet a part of me did not want the
   train to come
for with the whistle comes time
and time will bring me back here once
   more
smelling of a sea moving further away
   every minute
to walk across the platform to the other
   track, dragging my feet,
as limp in loss as the frond of seaweed
   in my pocket

Dave Calder

A Dream of Childhood

I dreamed a dream of childhood
Of candyfloss and sun
Of soaring kites and daisy chains
And endless hours of fun

Of sandcastles and rock pools
And swings and sherbet dips
Of pass the parcel, hide and seek
And Friday fish and chips

Of kicking leaves and conkers
Of sparklers in my hand
Of marshmallows and popcorn
And Christmas stockings crammed

Daniel Phelps

TRANSPORT

On the Train

When I look out of the window
on the train,
I can see sunshine,
I can see rain.
I can see horses
and the deep shining sea –
but then I see myself in the glass,
waving back at me!

Dave Ward

Bert

I think it very clever,
    and it took a lot of brains,
when engineers in days gone by
    invented railway trains.
But someone just as talented
    was Great-Great-Grandad Bert.
For he invented railway lines,
    cos trains can't run on dirt.

Barry Buckingham

Rocking Horse

I can
Joust in a tournament,
Ride into battle,
Slay a dragon,
Round up cattle,
Waylay a stagecoach,
Keep crowds at bay
Or just rock dreamily –
Who am I today?

Sue Cowling

How Did You Come to School?

"I rode on a pony," said Tony.
"I rode on a camel," said Hamel.
"That's nothing," said Jack.
"I rode on an elephant's back."

"I rode in a wagon
Pulled by a dragon," said Lee.
"That's nothing," said Tex.
"T rode on T-rex."

"I came in a canoe," said Sue.
"I rowed down the street," said Pete.
"That's nothing," said Dot.
"I came in a yacht."

"I came on a liner," said Dinah.
"I sailed on a pirate ship," said Pip.
"That's nothing," said Mark.
"I came on Noah's Ark."

"I flew in a jet," said Bet.
"I came in a balloon," said June.
"That's nothing," said Mac
"I came on an eagle's back."

"I came in a spaceship," said Dilip.
"I came in a UFO," said Jo.
"That's nothing," said Nick
"I came on my own broomstick."

"What about you, miss?" asked Chris.
Miss held up a silver thread and said,
"I came just after dawn
Riding on a unicorn."

John Foster

All Aboard

The night train leaves at midnight
From underneath the bed,
Its carriages are green and gold
Its engine is bright red.

Your name is on the driver's cab
In letters big and bold
And here's the hat you have to wear
And a scarf in case it's cold.

The passengers are every dream
You've ever had – and more –
So headlights on, blow the whistle,
Let the engine roar.

A trip to space? No problem!
A dive through oceans blue?
Push the button, make a wish
And watch it all come true.

For the night train runs on magic tracks,
It glides, it flies, it sails;
It spins through time and storyland,
Leaves shining silver trails.

So follow dolphins, dance with crabs,
Rollerskate with goats,
Helter-skelter down Mount Everest,
Race banana boats.

A hundred dreams are waiting
And the night train's still on track
To take you anywhere at all
And bring you safely back.

Patricia Leighton

If You Go Sailing Down the Nile

If you go sailing down the Nile
Beware the fearsome crocodile
Your holiday he'll try to scupper
By eating you up for his supper.

Richard Caley

Travel Details

Helicopters, racing cars.
Spacecraft sent
to study Mars.

Taxis, milk floats, trucks and trains.
Tractors chug
down country lanes.

Ships and trams and four-by-fours.
Whirring forklifts,
minus doors.

Motorbikes and submarines.
Wheels, propellers,
dials, machines.

Normal speed, so fast, quite slow.
Life's a journey,
on we go.

Stewart Henderson

Hot-Air Balloons Floating, Drifting, Turning

Floating
like huge, silent bath bubbles
above the summer greenness.
Drifting
against the red sky
like upturned water droplets.
Turning
gently with the wind's shallow breath
caressing their ribbed skins.

Hot-air balloons carry their
colours across the county.

Some day I'd like to travel in one:
lean out of the basket and
see the ponds below,
the fields,
see the woods,
the miniature castles.
See the toy-like cars slide along
Kent's straight Roman roads.

Most of all
I'd like to look down on my own village,
my own little house with its little red
    roof –
and facing the road, my own bedroom
    window.

If I saw it from above,
and I was floating, drifting, turning,
I'd think of the child
who lives there now and hope
he or she is happy; as I was living there
all those years ago.

Years before I was floating, drifting,
    turning.

John Rice

How to Get from A–Z

Ark,
Balloon,
Cruise,
Dodgem car,
Escalator – going far?
Ferry,
Glider,
Heliport,
Intercity,
Juggernaut.
Kart,
Lift,
Moped,
Narrowboat,
Oars,
Pram,
Quad bike,
Raft afloat!
Skateboard,
Taxi,
Underground,
Van,
Walk,

eXpress train,
  Yacht. Found
  Zeppelin to end my list.
(Bet you've thought of some I've
  missed!)

Sue Cowling

Sail Your Silver Boat

The sea is grey, the sky is black
The moon is paper white
Sail your lovely silver boat
Through the silver night
Sail your lovely silver boat
Through the silver night

The sea is green, the sky is blue
Sun shines yellow on the bay
Sail your lovely golden boat
Through the golden day
Sail your lovely golden boat
Through the golden day
Through the golden day.

Trevor Millum

WHERE WE LIVE

Setting Sail

I cast off when my light's out
And my bed's a boat once more,
Then hoist my sheet to catch the wind
And set sail from the shore.

Philip Waddell

Home Aroma

Some homes smell of dogs or cats.
Some homes smell of flowers.
Some smell ancient,
Some smell new.
But ours just smells like ours.

Kate Williams

In My Garden

What can you see in my garden?
What can you see on the wall?
Slugs and snails and caterpillars
And a spider learning to crawl.

What can you hear in my garden?
What can you hear from the tree?
Robins and thrushes and blackbirds –
You can hear them singing to me.

What can you find in my garden?
What can you find under a stone?
Ants and worms and woodlice
And a stag beetle living alone.

What can you smell in my garden?
What can you smell in the grass?
Lavender, lilies and roses –
You can smell them as you pass.

Moira Andrew

Secret Path

When I was your age,
Grandad told me,
There was a secret path

It ran along the edge
Of the allotments
Down the snake's back
Through the hawthorn trees
To the brickfields
And the dragon's lair

And there,
Grandad said,
We hid from the elves and trolls
And hatched plans
And ate our cheese and pickle
  sandwiches

Now the secret path
Is a housing estate
But the names of the roads . . .

Hawthorn Avenue
Snake Alley
Brick Lane
Elven Court
Dragon Close

Roger Stevens

High-Rise Views

I live in a block of flats
You can see for miles
The motorway smiles
And stretches like a cat.

Our flat is at the top
The lift sighs as it rises
It's full of surprises!
Until it reaches our stop.

We have flower boxes
With ivies and flowers
Flowers in the towers
Birds and no foxes.

When we go out to play
We have to descend
Drives you round the bend
All that way every day.

But at night what a sight!
Pink and red and orange light
Then whiteness of moonlight
Sleep tight at this height.

Ivan Jones

What a Racket!

Once upon a time
We lived in a house in town
And
THE CATS MIAOWED,
THE DOGS BOW-WOWED,
THE COLD WIND HOWLED,
THE LORRIES ROARED,
THE AIRCRAFT SOARED,
THE WINDOWS RATTLED
AND THE THUNDER CRASHED.

"The trouble with living in *town*," said
    Mum,
"is that it is SO noisy."
So we moved to the country –
And
THE CATS MIAOWED,
THE DOGS BOW-WOWED,
THE SHEEP WENT BAA,
THE COWS WENT MOO,
THE TRACTORS CHUGGED,
THE COLD WIND BLEW,
THE THUNDER CRASHED,

THE FIELD MICE SQUEAKED,
THE RAIN POURED DOWN,
THE HOUSE ROOF LEAKED.

"Lovely!" said Mum.
"There's nothing quite like *country*
  sounds!"

Trevor Harvey

Our Homes

I live in a street
made of snuggled-up houses
hear chattering feet

I live on a road
made of houses with hedges
hear rumbling loads

I live on a lane
with a farm and a cottage
hear birdsong and rain

Lynne Taylor

My Town

I climb to the top of the hill
Then look down at my town.
It's where I was born and live
The place where I have grown.
My big, busy, bustling world
From up here looks so small.
Though it has everything I love
My home, my friends and school.

Anne Sandell

Where Do You Live?

It might be a palace, or it might be a
  shed –
Have thirty rooms, or just one with a
  bed.
It might be a caravan, or a tent under
  the sky,
A bungalow, or a flat seven storeys
  high.
But I hope it's a place with a space of
  your own –
A place that's safe, a place to call
  home.

Tim Pointon

Living at the Seaside

We can hear the waves roar
when we're tucked in our beds
and we wake, not to traffic
but seagulls instead.
We can have picnics
down on the beach,
for we live in a cottage
just within reach
of the sand and the sea
and the rickety pier
and instead of just holidays,
we're here all year.

Marian Swinger

Where We Live

House
Castle
Igloo
Cottage
Caravan
Hut

Cave
Teepee
Terrace
Semi
Bungalow
Yurt

It really doesn't matter,
The name by which it's known.
For each and every one of us
It simply is our HOME.

Karen Costello-McFeat

WILDLIFE

We Share the Air . . .

With lions that roar,
With eagles that soar,
With wolves that howl
And dogs that growl,
With swifts that swoop
And loop the loop,
With foxes that bark
And the grinning white shark,
With slow-growing trees
And pollen-mad bees,
With nibbling black rats
And honey-eyed cats,
With seals and with snails
And spouting blue whales,
With dolphins that leap
And not too bright sheep,
With piglets and sows
And spiders and cows
So
Whether it's got roots
Or legs or flippers
Or wings,
Whether it swims

Or flies or slithers
Or sings,
Whether it's a fiery tiger
Or an angry wasp
With a red-hot sting:
We share the air with everything.

Kevin McCann

Wildlife

Our garden's full of wildlife –
it's nature in the raw.
Rocks and stones and dangers,
things that crawl and claw.
    We've stingers tall as steeples,
    butterflies and bugs,
    poppies bright as sunsets,
    flowers thick as rugs.
It's a jungle-land of tangles
skillywigs and bees,
scents as soft as roses,
others rich as cheese.
    We've radishes and sparrows,
    thistles sharp as spears,
    slugs as big as sea lions,
    snails with whopping ears.
My sister saw a tiger,
my brother smelt a fox
and life is so exciting
inside our

WINDOW BOX.

Peter Dixon

Noah's Last Words to the Animals

(Or a poem beginning with a line from a song)

See you later, alligator,
toodle-oo, kangaroo,
goodbye, wasp and fly,
so long, long-necked swan.

Take care, polar bear,
off you go, buffalo,
bye for now, brown cow,
drop me a line, porcupine.

Farewell, snail and shell,
good luck, goose and duck,
cheerie-bye, butterfly,
write to me, chimpanzee.

Lots of love, little dove.

David Horner

The Tiger

The
Tiger's just
A furry cat, he's
striped so be
aware
of that.

You must
be wary how

you greet him.
he's friendlier

when he's just
eaten. True

he never dines
alone, but says his

guests will sometimes
moan, that their smile

is often forced when
they become the

second

c
o
u
r
s
e

Sue Hardy-Dawson

Fox Wants a Hen

Fox wants a hen,
or a goose, or a vole.
Fox wants a rabbit
but rabbit's down its hole.
Fox wants a mouse.
She sees something squirm.
Fox pounces, gobbles.
Fox gets a . . . worm.

Marian Swinger

Up with the Dawn and the Dog and the Ducklings

Up with the dawn and the dog and the
    ducklings,
up with the dawn and the cat and the
    cow.
Swish all the swill to the pig and the
    piglings,
feed all the seed to the hen and the
    sow.

Clean up the cowshed, scrub out the
    stable,
brush up the barn and grub out the
    granary.
Heap all the hay to the height of the
    haystack,
stack all the cans at the back of the
    cannery.

Sleep in a heap in a shelter for
    sheeplings,
snort like a pony snoring
so loud.
Dream all the night about cheese sticks
    and chicklings,
dream all the day that you're caught in
    a cloud.

Up with the dawn and the dog and the
    ducklings,
up with the dawn and the cat and the
    cow.
Swish all the swill to the pig and the
    piglings,
feed all the seed to the hen and the
    sow.

John Rice

Elephacts

What do you call an elephant
   with a huge tummy?
                    A bellyphant.
What do you call an elephant
   who makes a lot of noise?
                    A yellephant.
What do you call an elephant
   who sells salads and salami?
                    A deliphant.
What do you call an elephant
   who likes jumping in puddles?
                    A wellyphant.
What do you call an elephant
   who can read and write?
                    A spellephant.
What do you call an elephant
   who loves watching TV?
                    A tellyphant.
What do you call an elephant
   when he's shaking with fear?
                    A jellyphant.

Alison Chisholm

A Proper Stickler!

Most fish show no parental care,
But the stickleback gets stuck in;
Guards the eggs, does StickleDad
While Mum goes off for a swim.

Bernard Young

Whalesong

I boom-mumble   I bass-blow
I hull-heavy   I big-slow
I boat-bump   I limpet-skin
I soft-sink   I sky-swim

I sea-search   I salt-swallow
I bone-backed   I fluke-follow
I gulf-cross   I listen-talk
I moon-map   I wave-walk

I tail-turn   I time-keep
I ship-wreck   I song-seek
I blue-blood   I grumble-sing
I fish-heart   I dream king

Sophie Stephenson-Wright

Aliens in the Pond

Planets of frogspawn
appear in the universe
of our garden pond.

Tadpoles are streaking,
beneath the still water, like
black-headed comets.

Two-legged creatures,
concealed in the pondweed, are
slowly transforming.

Speckle-skinned froglets
emerge, like green aliens
invading our earth!

Heather Reid

A Diminutive Frog

The tiniest frog you ever saw
is in the garden under the tomato
    plants.

She is a perfect miniature frog,
sludgy mottled brown and pond green
and you can see her little heart
beating, like the smallest pea, under
    her skin.

Her legs are longer than her body,
her feet are wider than her head.

I imagine the minuscule computer
of her brain
thinking minute froggy thoughts:
    how to find a croak
    to fit her fingerling body
    and how to catch a fly
    as big as a blackbird.

Judith Green

I Wasn't Me Tonight

I was a liquorice-black
velvet bat, arcing and
wheeling at twilight

slicing through the thin air
silent as silk.
My tight-skinned wings
stretched out against

the blossoming moon.

Matt Goodfellow

Index of First Lines

Index of Poets

Acknowledgements

The compiler and publisher wish to thank the following for permission to use copyright material:

Andrew, Moira, 'Imagine the World', 'Trudging through the Snow', 'Summer Picture', 'A Sense of Weather', 'In My Garden', by permission of the author; **Archer, Petonelle**, 'Follow Me', by permission of the author; **Barfield, Mike**, 'Where Am I?', 'Hush Now', by permission of the author; **Benson, Gerard**, 'Driving Home', by permission of the author; **Bevan, Clare**, 'The Princess's Treasures', first published in *Princess Poems*, Macmillan (2005), 'A Few Frightening Things', by permission of the author, 'Fairy Names', first published in *Fairy Poems*, Macmillan (2004), 'The Monster Under Your Bed', 'Beware of the . . . ?', 'Boring Mr Grimble', 'The Sound of Music', 'Sniff, Sniff . . .', by permission of the author, 'L is for Library', first published in *Read Me at School*, Macmillan (2009); **Boddy, Catharine**, 'Newborn', by permission of the author; **Bonner, Ann**, 'Moody', 'Music . . .', by permission of the author; **Brandling, Redvers**, 'Tummy Traveller', by permission of the author; **Brownlee, Liz**, 'Ladybird', by permission of the author; **Buckingham, Barry**, 'HELLO!', 'Bert', by permission of the author; **Burton, Philip**, 'Who Am I?', by permission of the author; **Calder, Dave**, 'Cargoes', 'Tillynaught Junction', by permission of the author; **Caley, Richard**, 'A Letter Home', 'Rainbow', 'If You Go Sailing Down the Nile', by permission of the author, 'Space Rocket', first published in *Time for a Rhyme – Magnificent Machines*, Macmillan (2000); **Carter, James**, 'Apple', 'What Are Dinos Made Of?', 'Derek the Dragon's Recipe for Damsel Pie', 'TheAncientGreeks . . .', 'On A Wild, Wild Walk . . .', by permission of the author, 'Show and Tell', first published in *Hey, Little Bug*, Frances Lincoln (2011), 'Goodbye Rhyme', by permission of the author, 'This is Where . . .', first published in *Journey to the Centre of My Brain*, Macmillan (2012); **Chisholm, Alison**, 'Peter's Pizzas', 'My Favourite Holiday', 'Elephacts', by permission of the author; **Clarke, Jane**, 'Sad–Happy', by permission of the author; **Coe, Mandy**, 'Small Mysteries', 'The Past Comes in Different Lengths', by permission of the author; **Cookson, Paul**, 'A Rainbow of Fruit Flavours', 'Who Am I?', 'Jerri the Gerbil's Workout Programme', 'Alliteration Space-Station Countdown', by permission of the author; **Corbett, Pie**, 'What Am I?', by permission of the author; **Costello-McFeat, Karen**, 'Nature Table', 'Where We Live', by permission of the author; **Cowling, Sue**, 'Jellybean, Bellybean', 'Pancake Chant', 'School Librarian', 'Dinner Lady', 'Urgent', 'The Great Fire', 'Remembrance', 'Hungry Wave',

'Rocking Horse', 'How to Get from A–Z', by permission of the author; **Davies, Brian**, 'Autumn Fields', by permission of the author; **Dean, Jan**, 'Everything's Better with You', first published in *Best of Enemies, Best of Friends,* ed. Ed Moses, Wayland (2011), 'Oh, Oh, the Story Man', 'Dentist', 'Excuse Me, Mrs Armitage, Can We Have Your Snow?', 'I Like the Way You Hop, Rabbit', 'Look', by permission of the author ,'Colouring In', first published in *Mice on Ice,* Macmillan (2004); **Denton, Graham**, 'Fossils', by permission of the author; **Dixon, Peter**, 'My Dad', 'Untraditional Pasty', 'Wisdom', 'Whelks and Winkles', 'Santa in Zooland', 'Sitting-Still Time', 'Holiday Swims', 'Wildlife', by permission of the author; **Douthwaite, Gina**, 'Puzzle the Puppy', by permission of the author; **Finney, Eric**, 'The Quiet Things', 'Weather Sense', 'Shells and Stones', by permission of the author, 'Cloud Dragon', first published in *Dolphins Leap Lampposts,* Macmillan (2002); **Floyd, Gillian**, 'The Apple', by permission of the author; **Foster, John**, 'My Baby Brother's Secrets', first published in *The Poetry Chest,* Oxford University Press (2007), 'Days', 'The Dinosaur Rap', 'Shiver Me Timbers! Yo-Ho-Ho!', 'It's A Pirate's Life for Me', 'How Did You Come to School?', by permission of the author; **Gallagher, Katherine**, 'Minibeasts', 'Our Class's Hamster Horatio', by permission of the author; **Gentles, Celia**, 'Baby Brother', 'Space', by permission of the author; **Gidney, Pam**, 'My Newt', by permission of the author; **Gittins, Chrissie**, 'Files Not Found on a Computer', by permission of the author; **Goodfellow, Matt**, 'A Complaint', 'I Wasn't Me Tonight', by permission of the author; **Green, Judith**, 'It's the Cougar in the Hoover', 'Red Admiral', 'Unicorns', 'Haiku Nightlight', 'A Diminutive Frog', by permission of the author; **Greygoose, David**, 'Lullaby', 'Fallen Leaves', 'Run to the Hilltop', by permission of the author; **Hardy-Dawson, Sue**, 'Spider-Man', 'The Tiger', by permission of the author; **Harmer, David**, 'Where the Fairies Are', 'How to Be a Pirate', '12 Ways to Spot a Pirate in Disguise', 'The Past', by permission of the author; **Harvey, Trevor**, 'What a Racket', first published in *Poetry Anthology,* ed. David Orme, Scholastic (1997) and as 'Sounds Familiar' in *Performance Poems,* ed. Brian Moses, Southgate (1996); **Henderson, Stewart**, 'Travel Details', by permission of the author; **Henry, Paul**, 'First Glasses', by permission of the author; **Horner, David**, 'Monisha', 'Noah's Last Words to the Animals', 'The Alphabite', by permission of the author; **Hughes, Paul**, 'Amelia the Pirate', by permission of the author; **Johnson, Mike**, 'Diary of a Butterfly', 'Autumnfall', by permission of the author; **Jones, Ivan**, 'High-Rise Views', by permission of the author'; **Joseph, Jenny**, 'Autumn, Winter, Spring, Summer', by permission of the author; **Langham, Tony**, 'I Can . . .', by permission of the author; **Leighton,**

Patricia, 'Listen and Look', 'All Aboard', by permission of the author; **Lockwood, Michael**, 'Playtime', by permission of the author; **Macdonald, Celina**, 'Beans v Peas', by permission of the author; **Macdonald, Violet**, 'Cream Curdled Oceans', 'Cowboys and Indians', 'Picking Poppies', by permission of the author; **Magee, Wes**, 'Gran's Old Diary', 'The Hairdresser's Questions', 'The Pirates are Walking the Plank', 'Pleasant Scents', by permission of the author; **Mayer, Gerda**, 'The Mermaids in the Sea', first published in *The Poetry Review* (1993), 'Tales', first published in *Gerda Mayer's Library Folder*, All-In 15 (1972); **McCann, Kevin**, 'If I Close My Eyes', 'We Share the Air . . .', by permission of the author; **Mellor, Robin**, 'Freddie's Little Sister', 'Sounds', by permission of the author; **Millum, Trevor**, 'Sail Your Silver Boat', by permission of the author; **Mole, John**, 'Jealousy', by permission of the author; **Morgan, Michaela**, 'Happy', 'Speaking Pirate', 'Sounds of School', by permission of the author; **Moses, Brian**, 'Twins?', 'Through the Dark', by permission of the author; **Nagle, Frances**, 'Oops', by permission of the author; **Peters, Jo**, 'Moving House', by permission of the author; **Phelps, Daniel**, 'A Dream of Childhood', PlanetPoetry.co.uk, by permission of the author; **Pointon, Tim**, 'Winter Night', 'Where Do You Live?', by permission of the author; **Rampton, Phil**, 'My Friends', 'My Past', by permission of the author; **Rawlinson, Julia**, 'The Seven Ages of a Leaf', 'The Past', by permission of the author; **Reid, Heather**, 'Aliens in the Pond', first published in *The Scrumbler* (issue 4 2012); **Rice, John**, 'The Faery Ferry', 'Dark Sky Lullaby', 'Up with the Dawn and the Dog and the Ducklings', by permission of the author, 'Hot Air Balloons Floating, Drifting, Turning', first published in *Red Lorry, Yellow Lorry*, ed. Fiona Waters, Macmillan (2007); **Rooney, Rachel**, 'Gravity', first published in *The Language of Cat*, Frances Lincoln (2011); **Rumble, Coral**, 'The Climber', 'At the Seaside', by permission of the author; **Saddler, Jane**, 'A Day at the Seaside', by permission of the author; **Sandell, Anne**, 'My Town', by permission of the author; **Sedgwick, Kate**, 'Mermaid's Purse', by permission of the author; **Sensier, Danielle**, 'my cat doesn't love, 'November Poem', 'New Year's Resolutions', by permission of the author; **Stephenson-Wright, Sophie**, 'Whalesong', by permission of the author; **Stevens, Roger**, 'I Am a Princess', 'Never Pick a Fight with a Fairy', 'I Did Not Eat the Goldfish', 'Pirates', 'Footprints', 'Holiday Scrap-Box', 'Secret Path', by permission of the author; **Swinger, Marian**, 'My Baby Sister', 'I Like Minibeasts', 'Lollipopped', 'Living at the Seaside', 'Fox Wants a Hen', by permission of the author; **Taylor, Lynne**, 'busy beeing lazy', 'black magic', 'Our Homes', by permission of the author; **Topping, Angela**, 'The Prayer of the Rabbits', first published in *'The New Generation* by Angela Topping,

313